IN SEARCH OF THE
Zeppelin
War

THE ARCHAEOLOGY OF
THE FIRST BLITZ

IN SEARCH OF THE
Zeppelin War

THE ARCHAEOLOGY OF THE FIRST BLITZ

DR NEIL FAULKNER
AND DR NADIA DURRANI

TEMPUS

Arthur Charles Faulkner (right) in his First World War flying kit. He is believed to have flown in two-seaters, and the other airman may, therefore, be his flying partner.

In loving memory of Neil's dad, Neil Charles Faulkner (1932–2007), who would have liked this book; his father, Neil's granddad, served in the Royal Flying Corps during the First World War.

Also in loving memory of Nadia's maternal grandfather, Georg Gaida (1909–45), an artist and German pacifist who was deported at the end of the Second World War and died en route to Siberia.

First published 2008

Tempus Publishing
Cirencester Road, Chalford
Stroud, Gloucestershire, GL6 8PE
www.thehistorypress.co.uk

Tempus Publishing is an imprint of The History Press

© Dr Neil Faulkner and Dr Nadia Durrani, 2008

The right of Dr Neil Faulkner and Dr Nadia Durrani to be identified as the Authors of this work has been asserted in accordance with the Copyrights, Designs and Patents Act 1988.

British Library Cataloguing in Publication Data.
A catalogue record for this book is available from the British Library.

ISBN 978 0 7524 4182 5

Typesetting and origination by The History Press
Printed and bound in Great Britain by Ashford Colour Press Ltd.

Contents

Introduction

Trench-war stalemate and endless battles of attrition in which thousands perished to capture a few yards of shell-blasted ground and mud-choked ditches: such are the images conjured by the First World War. Certainly, 'the war to end all wars' turned on great Western Front battles like the Somme, Verdun, and Passchendaele. The conflict, however, was global and multifaceted.

It was the first mass, industrialised 'total war', in which millions were conscripted to fight, and millions more were mobilised for production on the 'home fronts'. Whole economies and societies were transformed by a grinding year-on-year struggle. And while the war thundered in the Western Front, battles of equal importance were taking place on the Eastern Front between Russia on one side and Germany and Austria on the other. In addition, Northern Italy, the Balkans, and the Middle East constituted major secondary fronts. Moreover, the war was also fought at sea, especially in the grey wastes of the Atlantic and North Sea, where British warships maintained a blockade of Germany, while German U-boats attempted to choke British trade. And finally, it was fought in the sky.

The new war in the air was startling, frightening, and portentous. The war as a whole was not simply global in extent and 'total' in character and impact; it was also technological. Scientists and engineers worked constantly to improve equipment and weapons systems, and to steal a technological march on their countries' enemies. The air war was an especially dynamic branch of this novel techno-war.

Aircraft were first used primarily for reconnaissance. But their effectiveness – the speed at which they could cover ground and the breadth and extent of view they commanded – invited immediate attempts to shoot them down. The easiest way to do this was to send other aircraft against them, and a struggle for air supremacy began. Some visionaries had already predicted other uses for aircraft, however, either tactically, for ground attack in support of land-based operations, or even strategically, as an independent aerial bomber force attacking the enemy's industry, infrastructure, and civilian population.

At the beginning of 1915, Imperial Germany launched the first strategic bombing campaign in history. The target was Britain – its war industries, its essential services, its workforce, and above all, its capital city. Between January 1915 and August 1918, fifty-three bombing raids by Zeppelin airships were mounted, and between May 1917 and May 1918, there were thirty-three raids by Gotha and Giant aeroplanes. Though casualties and damage were limited, disruption and panic were widespread, and the British authorities were forced to construct the first home-defence system in history for resisting aerial attack. The bombers were countered by a string of coastal listening stations, a code-breaking department, an air-raid early warning system, rings of searchlights and anti-aircraft guns, and squadrons of home-defence fighter aircraft.

Strategic bombing has become an iconic form of war for modern humanity. We live in the shadow of Guernica, of London 1940, of the fire-bombing of Dresden and Hamburg, of the atomic explosions at Hiroshima and Nagasaki, and of the carpet-bombing of Vietnam and Cambodia. Millions died in the aerial bombing attacks of the twentieth century. And thousands are still dying, in the new twenty-first century, most recently, as we write, in Lebanon, Afghanistan, and Iraq.

This sort of war – indiscriminate mass killing of ordinary people from the air – was pioneered in the skies over London ninety years ago. Living memory of the conflict is fast disappearing. Those who witnessed the First Blitz as children are now in their nineties. Soon they will be gone, and the Zeppelins will be deep history, something from a time before anyone can remember. Though the First World War is relatively recent, accounts of it are not complete. Though much is lost forever, much else simply awaits rediscovery, locked in personal memory, forgotten in some archive, or surviving in the landscape as an overgrown ruin of brick and concrete.

In 2005 our newly formed Great War Archaeology Group (GWAG) set out to investigate the evidence for the first strategic bombing campaign

'Who art thou that judgest another mans servant.' In a corner of the churchyard at Theberton is this burial plaque dedicated to the German aircrew who died in the destruction of Zeppelin L48 – victims of a new kind of war in the skies over Britain.

in history. This book is the story of that project. It is an account of what we have found out so far about the First Battle of Britain. It is also an appeal to others to get involved in researching, conserving and displaying Britain's largely unrecorded, much neglected, and fast degrading First World War archaeological heritage – because it is a past that matters, a past that we need to understand, a past that can help us, if we learn its lessons, to make the future better.

Dr Nadia Durrani
Dr Neil Faulkner
London
September 2007

1

The Destruction of Zeppelin L48

By 2.30 on the morning of 17 June 1917, the German Zeppelin L48, flying north along the coast beyond Harwich, was in trouble. One of a new generation of super 'height-climber' Zeppelins, L48 was on its maiden bombing mission to Britain. The mission was doomed from the start. Six Zeppelins had been assigned to the raid, but two had been prevented from leaving their sheds by stiff crosswinds, and two others had been forced to return home early with engine trouble. Only L42 and L48 had made it to the British coast. They got no further. A thunderstorm raged inland, and all hope of reaching London, the principal target of opportunity, was quickly abandoned: the weather had blown shut the small window of time given to the airships to complete their mission.

For Zeppelins were machines of the night — stealth-bombers that relied, ideally, on the darkness of long moonless nights for safety, often launching their bombing runs with engines shut down, drifting silently with the wind, the underbellies of the latest models camouflaged with black paint. Yet Peter Strasser, Germany's iron-hard airship commander-in-chief, had ordered this raid with the shortest night of the year less than a week away. Some had doubted his wisdom. Some considered the mission little short of suicidal. With only a few hours of half-light, the airships could not afford to linger over enemy territory, for to be caught in daylight would be to fall almost certain prey to Britain's increasingly efficient and numerous home-defence fighter aircraft.

Height-climbers like L42 and L48 had been developed in direct response to this threat. The previous autumn, in the space of just a month, four state-of-the-art airships had been shot down by British night-fighters. The

The L48 at Friedrichshafen in May 1917. The mighty Zeppelin was 645ft long – more than two football pitches in length, or three Jumbo 747s nose-to-tail. Having been stripped of every bit of excess weight possible to help it climb higher, it weighed in at just over 25 tons – whereas the average Jumbo weighs 390 tons at take-off. Such was L48's volume that it could have held 687,400 gallons of water – the equivalent of more than eighteen Olympic-size swimming pools. (D.H. Robinson via Ray Rimell)

German High Command, though badly shaken, had kept its nerve and resolved to invest in a new generation of machines able to reach altitudes beyond the range of the British defences. Everything that could be done in the new design to reduce weight was done. The old three-engine rear gondola with outrigger brackets for propellers was replaced by a twin-engine version powering a single propeller. Fuel capacity was cut from 36 to 30 hours' flying time. The number of bomb release mechanisms was halved. The hull structure was lightened. The control gondola became more compact. All accommodation and comforts for the crew were eliminated. This new generation of Zeppelins – the 'Forties' – were thus able to reach altitudes above 20,000ft, around 3,000ft higher than their predecessors, the 'Thirties'.

The height-climbers had made their debut over Britain on 16 March 1917. There had been problems from the beginning. Four miles up, higher than any aviators had ever ascended, the German aircrew entered

A model of L48. Note the tiny size of the gondolas suspended below the Zeppelin's huge canopy. The forward one was the control gondola, the rear one the main engine gondola, the two small ones amidships also engine gondolas.

L48 in 'night camouflage' on a trial flight. As home defences improved, the undersides of Zeppelins were painted with black dope to make it harder for enemy searchlights to pick them up.

An official military shot of L48, showing the two amidships engine gondolas, and the black cross of Imperial Germany.

Zeppelin Wreck. East Anglia. June 17th. 1917.

A contemporary postcard showing the wreckage of L48 in Crofts Field at Theberton Hall Farm – a tangled mass of lightweight duralumin girders.

the eerie world of the sub-stratosphere. Here, machines were buffeted by gales unknown to weather stations on the ground. Engines seized up, metalwork shattered, and instruments failed in the bitter cold. The aircrew were afflicted by pounding headaches, nausea, exhaustion, and frostbite. Moreover, from their icy nocturnal perches, the Zeppelin captains could discern almost nothing of the ground, and both navigation and targeting became little more than lotteries. The average damage inflicted by a raider slumped from around £6,500 in summer 1916 to around £2,000 now.

Thus, in the early hours of 17 June, with the pale glow of dawn already showing in the east, L48 was in trouble. Approaching the East Anglian coast around midnight, in the bitter cold at 18,000ft, first the starboard engine had failed, then the forward engine had begun knocking badly, and finally the magnetic compass had frozen. Giving up on London, Kapitänleutnant Franz Georg Eichler ordered a bombing run over Harwich prior to turning for home. But the twenty-four recorded bombs dropped by L48 that night all landed harmlessly in Suffolk fields.

By then, the home defence was on full alert. During the bombing run, two dozen searchlights had snapped on, thrusting long, luminous, groping arms into the night sky. Then one of the arms caught the airship and held it in a circle of light. The others had quickly closed into a tight cone, bathing the airship in bright, dazzling light, illuminating its black underbelly, strung with tiny gondolas, and emblazoned with the serial number and the black cross of Imperial Germany. 'Instantly it began to thunder and lightning below,' recalled Leutnant zur See Otto Mieth, the airship first officer, 'as if an inferno had been let loose. Hundreds of guns fired simultaneously, their flashes twinkling like fireflies in the blackness beneath. Shells whizzed past and exploded. Shrapnel flew. The ship was enveloped in a cloud of gas, smoke, and flying missiles.'

Fear twisted inside every man aboard. Weariness, the cold, the constant gasping for air were subsumed by the imminence of the fate most feared by men who fight in the air: burning to death in a tangle of flaming wreckage. For what was an airship but a vast gas-filled incendiary bomb? L48 flew only because it was lighter than air. A huge lightweight framework of duralumin girders and steel wires supported a row of eighteen gas-bags made of animal membrane, cotton fabric, and glue, which, when inflated, contained two million cubic feet of hydrogen gas and filled almost the entire interior space. Stretched over the exterior of the framework was an envelope of light cotton fabric, coated in dope, laced together, and pulled taut. The keel of the duralumin framework formed a gangway running the length of the ship, and here were stowed water-ballast sacks, petrol tanks, and bomb racks. Slung beneath the keel were the forward control gondola and three engine gondolas, a large one towards the rear, two smaller ones amidships. The airship's five engines (with two in the rear gondola) powered four propellers, one at the back of each gondola, and afforded a maximum speed of 67mph. Direction was controlled by cables which ran from the forward gondola to movable rudders and elevators attached to the ends of the four tail-fins.

At almost 200m long and 24m across, L48 was bigger than a battleship. She was, at once, a triumph of modern engineering, a symbol of

The contorted wreckage of L48 captured in another contemporary postcard. Amid the structural girders are two sections of ladder by which aircrew would have moved between the gondolas and the hull. Commemorative or 'newsy' postcards such as this were commonplace at that time.

industrialised war, and a sinister black force in the night sky threatening death and destruction to those below. For the men who served her she was also something more: a huge, slow-moving, technically unreliable and highly vulnerable flying machine, with the potential to be transformed in an instant into a vast celestial funeral pyre.

There were nineteen men aboard that night. Half were machinists serving the engines, which required constant maintenance and occasional in-flight repairs. Though warmed by the engines during the long hours of flight, a head-splitting roar and an asphyxiating mix of oil and exhaust fumes assailed the machinists. Meanwhile, in the forward control gondola, bitter cold assailed the airship's three officers – Korvettenkapitän Viktor Schütze, the commander of naval airships and leader of the raid, Kapitänleutnant Eichler, the commander of L48, and Leutnant zur See Mieth, his executive officer. Also in the control car were two petty officers operating rudders and elevators, two more working in a soundproof wireless compartment, and a navigator. Despite it being high summer, temperatures could sink below -25°C. The crew wore thick woollen underwear, blue naval uniforms, leather overalls, fur overcoats, scarves, goggles, leather helmets, thick gloves of leather and wool, and large felt overshoes covering their boots. They were sustained by generous rations of bread, sausage, stew, chocolate, and thermos flasks of strong coffee. Thus did the pioneers of military aviation enter the strange new combat zone of the upper skies.

L48 completed its bombing run unscathed. She then dropped to 13,000ft and headed for home. But the frozen compass misled the navigator, and instead of setting a course east, L48 went north, along rather than away from the British coast. By the time the error was detected, the forward engine had failed, and the airship's speed, dependent now on three engines, was well down. Eichler radioed stations in the German Bight for bearings, and with them came the information that he would find useful tailwinds to assist his speed if he descended to 11,000ft. But the telephone lines that fed information from radio stations and observer posts to home-defence headquarters on the ground, and from there to the searchlights, AA batteries, and fighter airfields, were already humming. The lower skies were filling with hostile aircraft as they brightened with approaching dawn.

A postcard showing the wreckage of L48 in Crofts Field, including the hedge which was later grubbed out, guarded by soldiers.

Military salvage team at work on the debris of L48. The wreckage was of huge importance to the war effort, providing much information about the workings of the Zeppelins. The salvage teams reduced the wreck to manageable sizes for transporting by road to a special goods-train at Leiston Rail Station (three miles away). From there the remains were taken to The Royal Aircraft Establishment (or RAE) at Farnborough, where it was hoped valuable data could be collected to help Britain in her own efforts at designing successful military and civil airships.

At 1.55a.m. Second Lieutenant Frank Holder and Sergeant Sydney Ashby ascended from the Royal Flying Corps airfield at Orfordness in an FE2b night-fighter (see image on page 61). Built of wood, wire and canvas, First World War aircraft were flimsy, low-powered, and often lethally dangerous to fly. As well as being slow, difficult to manoeuvre, and liable to develop technical faults in flight, they could take up to half an hour to climb to maximum altitude. The FE2b had a maximum speed of 92mph, an altitude ceiling of 11,000ft, and could stay in the air for only two hours thirty minutes. A pusher-biplane, with engine and propeller behind the cockpit, it had the appearance of a huge bug, with a stubby, round-nosed fuselage, and open struts and wires connecting this to the tail-plane. An observer sat in the nose, the pilot in a raised cockpit behind, and both were armed with machine-guns.

Holder first sighted L48 at about 2.10a.m., during her bombing run over Harwich under heavy anti-aircraft fire. The British had already developed a distinctive air-war doctrine: air supremacy – and thereby security from aerial bombardment – was to be achieved by relentless efforts to locate and destroy enemy aircraft. The British fighters were hunter-killers: once an airship had been sighted, their job was to pursue and attack just as long as they had operational range. Holder now did exactly that. He attempted to close with L48 over Harwich, but he could not achieve the necessary height, his and Ashby's fire was ineffective, and his own machine-gun promptly jammed.

Following as L48 headed north, however, Holder began to gain on the airship as she was slowed by engine failure and descended in an effort to gain speed. Two other British fighters were also closing in. Flight Commander Henry Saundby had taken off from Orfordness at 2.55a.m. in a DH2 pusher-biplane (see image on page 64). The DH2 had a similar bug-like appearance to Holder's FE2b, but it was a single-seater, considerably smaller – with a wingspan of only 8.5m as against 14.5m – and performed rather better. Meantime, Second Lieutenant 'Don' Watkins had taken off from Goldhanger in a BE12 (see image on page 62). A conventional single-seater aircraft with engine and propeller at the front, the BE12 was exceptionally stable, affording the pilot, who had to control the plane while doubling as machine-gunner, a secure firing platform amid the vagaries of aerial combat.

There were several other planes up, but only Holder, Saundby and Watkins actually engaged the Zeppelin. Around 90 per cent of home-defence pilots never saw their enemy in the air; of the minority who did, only a handful got close enough to engage. It was a combination of spreading light that June morning and the stricken and befuddled condition of their prey that allowed no less than three British fighters to join the kill.

As Holder closed, his observer fired off several drums of ammunition, the last at a range of just 300 yards, before Holder twisted the machine away. Someone else was also firing. Saundby had come up under the airship's tail and fired off three drums at rapidly shortening ranges. Watkins also came in under the swaying tail, firing off a drum at long range, climbing steeply to close and fire off another, then finally bringing his plane to within 150 yards of the monster and firing three short bursts to empty a drum before veering away.

Two miles up in the half-light of dawn, blasted by bitter cold in their open cockpits, four British airmen were engaged in a new kind of combat, as tiny machines of wood, wire and canvas flew around a giant of the air twenty-five times bigger, spitting fire at her. The upward-firing Lewis gun was the decisive weapon, but only since the development of specialised incendiary bullets filled with phosphorous. These had the capacity to ignite escaping hydrogen as it mixed with air once a gas-bag had been punctured. As Holder turned away and looked back, he saw that L48 had begun to burn. His watch told 3.25a.m. Saundby and Watkins also saw fire. All three pilots hauled their machines clear: they knew that the fire would become a raging inferno in seconds, able to torch anything near it in the sky.

Thousands more had been watching down below, alerted by the searchlights and guns around Harwich, by the dull boom of the airship's bombs, by the hum of escaping airship and pursuing fighters, and then, as the sky lightened, by the spectacle of the aerial combat unfolding above them. Motorcycling along a local road at about 3.15a.m. that morning, Captain Dimmock had seen the Zeppelin heading for the coast, under fire from an aeroplane pursuing at great distance. He could see the Zeppelin clearly against the reddish tint in the sky, swaying gently from side to side, as if underpowered. Then there were flashes of fire from what Dimmock guessed was a second attacking plane, apparently causing the Zeppelin to turn several times as its commander took evasive action.

Schoolboy George Foster was also watching, from his home in the village of Saxmundham. He guessed, from the knocking sound within, that the Zeppelin was in trouble as it drifted towards the North Sea. Then he too saw a fighter attack, as a British plane passed the Zeppelin, made a turn, and then fired two short bursts. Young housewife Doris Peecock, also a resident of the village, was awakened by:

> … the strangest noise I had ever heard … as if a mighty traction engine had somehow got up into the air and was ploughing an irregular course through the sky … an enormous Zeppelin, lumbering and disabled, was literally staggering across the sky. It was quite low down and obviously suffering from engine trouble. The noise was deafening, and even as we gazed an aeroplane appeared out of the sky and started manoeuvring round and round the staggering 'Zepp', firing as it flew.

From start to finish, the aerial combat lasted for perhaps ten minutes. As it raged round them, the German aircrew, trapped inside their clanking machine, were filled with foreboding. Then, suddenly, the control gondola was flooded with light. For a moment it was as if the airship had again been caught in the beam of a searchlight. Leutnant zur See Otto Mieth, glancing up, saw that the underbelly was on fire.

> Almost instantly our 600 feet of hydrogen was ablaze. Dancing, lambent flames licked ravenously at her quickly bared skeleton, which seemed to grin jeeringly at us from the sea of light. So it was all over.

Mieth threw off his overcoat, thinking to swim if the airship landed in the sea. Korvettenkapitän Schütze stood calm and motionless, his eyes fixed momentarily on the flames above, staring death steadfastly in the face. Then he turned to bid Mieth farewell and announced, 'It's all over.'

For several seconds no one moved or spoke in the gondola. There was just the roar of flames as each man grasped that the end had come. Their greatest fear was to burn inside the fireball either as it dropped through the sky or pinioned on the ground amid red-hot metal and flaming canvas. Airship crew openly discussed such dangers in their mess-rooms, and most agreed it was best to jump. Mieth now sprang to one of the side-windows of the gondola, intent on leaping out. Before he could do so:

More men at work on the wreckage, the huge quantity of which is apparent. But how comprehensive was their salvage? Did they leave behind anything of L48 in the field where it fell just outside the little village of Theberton? That is what the Great War Archaeology Group set out to discover in the summer of 2006.

A postcard showing the tail end of L48 standing upright in Crofts Field. It has clearly been moved away from the main mass of wreckage prior to being loaded onto a lorry for transport to the local railway station.

> ... a frightful shudder shot through the burning skeleton and the ship gave a convulsion ... the gondola struts broke with a snap, and the skeleton collapsed with a series of crashes like the smashing of a huge window.

The strain on the vast framework of girders and wires as the supporting hydrogen burnt off had caused it to buckle and shatter amidships. The rear engines now acted as a giant weight, twisting the flaming wreckage into a lop-sided V-shape, the mass of the hull falling vertically through the sky on one side, the tail-plane on the other.

> Flames and gas poured over us as we lay there in a heap. It grew fearfully hot. I felt flames against my face, and heard groans. I wrapped my arms about my head to protect it from scorching flames, hoping the end would come quickly. That was the last I remember.

Machinist's Mate Heinrich Ellerkamm had just climbed the ladder from his station in the port engine gondola onto the gangway inside the hull when disaster struck. He had heard machine-gun fire, seen a British plane, and watched fascinated as the flaming phosphorous bullets ripped into the airship's fabric. He heard a dull 'woof' like a gas oven lighting, then saw a burst of flames, and almost immediately one gas-bag after another was exploding into flame over his head. Terrified that he might be trapped beneath the wreckage when it hit the ground, he tried to climb up the girders.

> Flames were dancing everywhere, and the heat was overpowering. My fur coat collar caught fire; I tried to beat it out with my hands. The weight of the big aft two-engine gondola was dragging down the stern, the ship tipped vertically and down we plunged, a monstrous roaring banner of flame reaching hundreds of metres above my head, and the wind whistling through the bared framework. I noticed the draft was driving the flames away from me.

The watching thousands on the ground saw it all. First the tail section had taken on the classic 'Chinese lantern' appearance as the outer envelope was illuminated from within by fire. Then, as the burning gas became an inferno, a series of huge white incandescent fireballs lit up the sky as the gas-bags exploded. As flames streaked up the sides of the airship, massive sheets of highly doped envelope-fabric were ripped apart and blasted into the sky. As they were consumed, these flaming fragments left trails of smoke in the air. Millions of tiny greasy black smuts were created from the burning fabric and spread by the wind across miles of countryside.

The main mass of wreckage – a vast tangle of red-hot girders and wires, thousands of tatters of flaming fabric, broken gondolas and engines creaking and grinding, a torch of fire trailing hundreds of feet into the air behind, a handful of men cowering and burning – took three or four minutes to fall. Doris Peecock was mesmerised:

> Then began the awful descent of the monster, terrible to witness as we stood shivering in the chill dawn of a June morning. Piece by piece burning fabric floated down, and still the strange craft, now mortally wounded, staggered on. I thought of those poor wretches, trapped in those red-hot gondolas… That is war in the air, a nightmare horror.

Zeppelin L48 crashed in a field at Theberton Hall Farm. The rear engines smashed heavily into the ground and the base of the V-shape into which the superstructure had been contorted in the air crumpled on top like a concertina. Residual gas, fuel and oil exploded into a huge tower of flames. But the bow remained intact and erect, rising majestically beyond the shattered remains of stern and middle hull, as the wreckage continued for some time to burn and smoke.

Otto Mieth, still beneath the bodies of his comrades in the control gondola, was shaken back to consciousness by the concussion. 'I remember a thrill of horror as I opened my eyes and saw myself surrounded by a sea of flames and red-hot metal beams and braces that seemed about to crush me.' He then lost consciousness again, recovering only after his rescue by local civilians and soldiers, hurrying rapidly to the scene of destruction.

Heinrich Ellerkamm, clinging to the girders of the main framework, also felt the impact:

> Suddenly there was a terrible, continuous roaring smashing of metal as the
> stern struck the ground and the hull structure collapsed beneath me. I found
> myself on the ground with the breath half knocked out of me, the framework
> crashing down on top of me, fuel and oil tanks bursting on impact and their
> burning contents flowing towards me through the shattered wreckage. I was
> trapped in a tangle of red-hot girders, the heat roasting me alive through my
> heavy flying coat. If I had lost consciousness I would have burned to death.

Ellerkamm prised apart red-hot girders and never felt the pain in his hands till later. He was found afterwards wandering across the field in a daze.

Machinist's Mate Wilhelm Uecker also survived, trapped in the wreckage of the starboard engine gondola, from which he was rescued by civilians and carried away on a stretcher. The rest of the crew were dead. Several had jumped from the forward gondola, including Viktor Schütze, who was found with his legs buried up to his knees in the ground, and Franz Eichler, whose body was among a group of five found lying in a cornfield a few hundred yards from the wreckage. The rest had burned to death, either during the descent or after crashing. Bodies were pulled from the forward engine area still burning. Others lay beneath heaps of smoldering, twisted metal, and took longer to recover. Three blackened corpses were eventually removed from beneath the rear gondola.

Great swathes of L48 wreckage lay across Crofts Field. Perhaps the tent was some sort of temporary site office.

Bit by bit, the wreckage of L48 was cut up, pulled apart and removed from the site. In this shot the work of the salvage team seems well advanced.

Crofts Field was a battleground. The wreckage of L48 was that of a fallen foe. The men of this military salvage team are the victors. The man to the far left smiles beguilingly to the camera while striking an (understandably) jaunty, triumphant pose. Behind lies the gnarled debris of the ultimate 'baby-killer', the height-climbing super-Zeppelin L48, including the great nose-cone, still standing erect.

It had been L48's maiden mission, and she had carried the commander of the naval airship fleet. The day before, the Nordholz station band had played 'Admiral of the Air' as L48 was hauled from her shed, but the mid-day heat had cracked the skin of the big drum. Then the men onboard recalled that this was their thirteenth mission together, having previously crewed L11. Now sixteen were dead, another would die shortly of his wounds, and only two would see Germany again.

Kapitänleutnant Martin Dietrich, commander of L42, the only other Zeppelin to raid Britain that night, had witnessed the destruction of his comrades-in-arms from a distance and radioed the news to Leader of Airships Peter Strasser. When L42 came in, Strasser was out on the field to meet it. He climbed aboard and demanded details. It took some persuasion for him to believe that L48 had fallen victim to fighter attack.

But Dietrich was insistent, and Strasser left dejected and temporarily broken, remaining in his quarters for the rest of the day. The height-climbers had suffered a decisive defeat. The great smoking heap of metal debris at Theberton Hall Farm signalled the end of the Zeppelin as a strategic bomber.

The British authorities were soon at the scene, taking charge of prisoners, recovering bodies and documents, and setting up a cordon around the wreckage to keep at bay hundreds of sightseers and souvenir-hunters. To the general public, the downed airship was a mix of battle debris, military trophy, technological curiosity, and, for some at least, commercial opportunity. For the authorities, on the other hand, it was an intelligence asset, one whose every fragment was to be recovered for forensic examination. An early coup was the recovery from the smashed control gondola of lists and tables of German naval codes. Soon, officers of the Admiralty's Constructional Department arrived to take charge of the salvage operation. First, the entire wreck, despite its distorted form, was carefully measured *in situ*. Then, the parts were chopped into manageable sizes, loaded onto motor-trucks, and sent to Leiston railway station for transport out of the area.

But the authorities did not recover everything. Some locals had made off with chunks of Zeppelin before the military cordon had been established. Access was then restricted by the erection of two fences around the wreck. Soon the nearby lane was cleared of civilian vehicles, two picket lines of soldiers were posted, and all remaining spectators were ushered from the field. But some of those allowed inside the cordon took the opportunity to collect souvenirs or pilfer items for sale. Several staff officers were seen departing with bits of wreckage. Further opportunities were afforded the dedicator collector or dealer as small fragments fell off the loaded trucks in the country lanes between Theberton Hall Farm and Leiston station. Finally, after weeks of official salvage, once the military had departed with their spoil, the souvenir-hunters moved in to pick over the site for any micro-debris that had been missed.

By late summer, Theberton's 'Zeppelin Field' was reduced to a vivid memory and a set of grainy photographs. Of L48 itself – some 200m of girders, wires, and fabric – nothing whatsoever remained.

Or so it seemed.

2

In Search of the Zeppelin War

Almost ninety years after the destruction of Zeppelin L48, on Friday 14 April 2006, a small team of metal-detectorists led by Julian Evan-Hart were on the site of the crash in Crofts Field at Theberton Hall Farm. The locale remains much the same. At the top of the field runs a farm track. From here the ground slopes down to a wood. Some of the trees, both in the wood and in nearby hedgerows, could be recognised as more mature versions of young trees visible in air photographs of the Zeppelin wreckage taken in June 1917. There were, then, some landmarks to help orientation, but the air photographs were all obliques, so it is not possible to plot from them the precise location of the crash. The hedge against which the fallen Zeppelin had lain has been grubbed out, converting the former two fields into a single 5.5-hectare D-shaped one. With the most important landmark in a large field gone, finding anything that remained of L48 was not going to be easy.

The metal-detector was to prove decisive in the search. Its history of use in archaeology is chequered and controversial. Some archaeologists remain deeply hostile to both the tool and those who use it, largely on the basis that some metal-detectorists, especially the so-called 'nighthawks', are simply looters out for gain. But most metal-detected discoveries have little monetary value. Routine Roman coins sell for a few pounds at the most, and even the small minority of hardened criminals who are regularly out at night detecting on freshly ploughed fields intent on stealing our past will probably never strike it rich. Instead, most detectorists – of whom there are probably around 15,000 in Britain – are simply hobbyists interested in history. The objects recovered are

Crofts Field at Theberton Hall Farm in Suffolk in the summer of 2006. This was the crash site of Zeppelin L48. But where exactly did L48 fall? It was the job of Julian Evan-Hart's metal-detecting team to find out. (Nadia Durrani for GWAG)

important not for their commercial value, but because they allow the finder to 'touch the past'.

Julian Evan-Hart is a veteran detectorist. He is also an experienced aviation archaeologist, and an expert on the material debris of modern warfare. His seriousness is measured by the fact that he is a leading member of the Great War Archaeology Group (GWAG). His mission that April Friday was not simply to search for bits of Zeppelin in the plough-soil, but to locate a crash site for future excavation by a full archaeological team.

A preliminary detector sweep can be carried out fast. Julian was convinced that an event as massive as the destruction of L48 could not fail to leave a 'metal signature' in the ground: numerous small bits of metal from the wreckage that had been missed or ignored by the salvage teams and souvenir-hunters of 1917.

Metal-detectors represent a technology unavailable in the First World War – they are a development from Second World War mine-detectors.

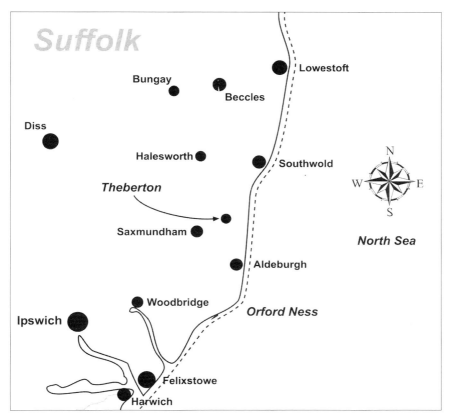

Map of the Theberton area of Suffolk showing major settlements and sites involved in the aerial combat on the night of 16–17 June 1917. (Dave Hibbitt for GWAG)

Relatively cheap detectors for hobbyists first became widely available in the 1970s. The search head of a detector contains a transmitter which generates a ground-penetrating electro-magnetic field. Metal objects in the ground disrupt that field and create a localised disturbance that can be picked up by antennae, also located in the search head, and then amplified by the detector's circuitry. This disturbance is then turned into an audio or visual signal that the operator receives either through head-phones or by observing the monitor on the machine's control-box.

Detectorists are looking for particular types of object. A recent survey showed that 98 per cent of metal objects in plough-soil are of iron, and 75 per cent of these are nails. To avoid being bogged down digging large amounts of metallic junk, modern metal-detectors are equipped with

Metal-detectorist Martin Plummer sweeps the barley field at Theberton with his high-tech detector, looking for tell-tale fragments of L48. (Nadia Durrani for GWAG)

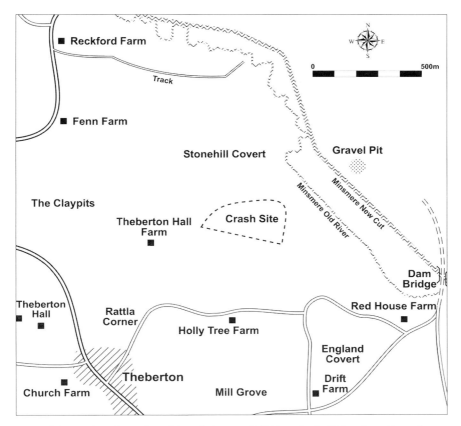

Map of the D-shaped Crofts Field at Theberton Hall Farm in Suffolk, where Zeppelin L48 crashed to earth. (Dave Hibbitt for GWAG)

a discriminator that allows the operator to 'knock out' ferrous signals. Different metals have different conductivity and therefore disrupt the electro-magnetic field in different ways. Iron is highly conductive and gives strong signals, so you can set the discriminator to exclude much of it. But there are limits. The discriminator can be set to exclude objects ranging from, at one extreme, small iron nails to, at the other, aluminium ring-pulls. Most detectorists set it close to the bottom of the range because anything higher risks losing finds. There is a 'safe level' for the discriminator so as not to exclude the weak signals given off by small non-ferrous objects lying at depth. If you want to detect a small piece of aluminium 6in down, you will probably need a setting that will also pick up a large nail at the same depth.

On this occasion, the detectorists played safe: they did not want to miss anything, so they set their machines for 'all metals'. Anticipating tiny fragments of metallic debris, some perhaps at depth, they had to keep their discriminators open. That way, if there was any significant quantity of metal debris in the plough-soil at the crash site, the detectors would pick it up. Each man was also equipped with a small, short-handled spade. When his detector registered a 'target', he would dig out the soil beneath, checking continually to establish whether the signal was still coming from the ground or was now in the growing pile of displaced soil around the hole. Once the target was out, the loose soil would be run under the detector-head a handful at a time, until finally the object was isolated and recovered.

The soil conditions were not good. Much of the chalk bedrock that underlies most of East Anglia is buried beneath extensive spreads of mixed sand and gravel – fluvio-glacial moraines dumped by dynamic rivers of melt-water at the end of a great ice age half a million years ago. The sand is acidic, and the soils formed of it are corrosive. And aluminium, the basic ingredient of the alloy duralumin from which the giant girders of L48 were built, is especially prone to degrade, not least when severely burnt. On the other hand, moisture and agro-chemicals tend to leach away faster in sandy soils, protecting metal objects somewhat from these other agents of corrosion. What would be the balance of preservation and decay in Crofts Field after ninety years?

Halfway down the field, in an area where the crop of growing barley seemed stunted, the detectors were buzzing. Contemporary air photographs implied that this was approximately the right spot. Everything seemed to fit. An aviation crash could pollute the soil for decades, having subjected it to searing heat, doused it with oil and petrol, and filled it with corroding aluminium fragments. The area of stunted growth measured about 25m across: roughly the diameter of an airship that had crumpled up on itself lengthways. In the centre of the spread was an area where the detectors were registering targets with every sweep: surely the epicentre of the crash site, the point at which L48's rear engines had plunged into the ground, trailing the vast burning skeleton of twisted airframe behind them.

But did any of it really matter? So much was already known about the destruction of L48 that night in June 1917. Two of the German aircrew had left memoirs. The British fighter pilots had made official reports. The observations of various eyewitnesses on the ground had been written

A triumphant Julian Evan-Hart holds up a minute fragment of L48 that he has just metal-detected. (Nadia Durrani for GWAG)

down and preserved. The wreckage had been photographed from several angles in the air, and there were numerous detailed shots taken at ground-level. Both German and British records survive which allow the design of L48 to be faithfully reconstructed. What more is there to be known? What is the point of archaeological investigation? Are First World War archaeologists not simply digging for the fun of it?

The archaeology of the First World War – and of modern industri-alised conflict generally – is relatively new. The casual or deliberate collection of war debris – and sometimes its fashioning into distinctive 'trench art' objects – has a long history. The fate of the debris of L48 is an example of that – with bits of the wreckage being turned into curiosities such as an umbrella stand. More recently, there have been amateur digs to investigate war sites and recover military artefacts, especially on parts of the former Western Front in Northern France and Belgian Flanders. And there has been much straightforward battlefield looting to feed the militaria fairs and internet sales sites. But systematic research by qualified archaeologists was almost unknown until about fifteen years ago, when first in France, then in Belgium, state-employed professionals began to get involved in the archaeology of the Western Front.

There are now at least two specialist First World War groups in Britain led by a mix of professional, academic and independent archaeologists. One is the longer-established No Man's Land, which has worked mainly on the Somme in Northern France and on the sites of former training camps and practice trenches on Salisbury Plain and elsewhere in Britain; the other is the Great War Archaeology Group (GWAG).

GWAG was set up in 2004 by Neil Faulkner (one of the editors of this book) and David Thorpe. Faulkner is a freelance academic archaeologist who works as a writer, lecturer, and field director. Thorpe is a veteran of the professional archaeology circuit who has worked for *Time Team*, the Museum of London, and several Mediterranean excavations. For both men, GWAG represents the fusion of a fascination with modern mili-tary history and a passion for archaeological fieldwork. Might not the skills of archaeologists be applied to advance knowledge, understanding and awareness of the First World War – a war now on the cusp of living memory, soon to be consigned to the realm of pure 'history', soon to be beyond the reach of any human's personal recollection?

There was something more: some of the leading members of the group had an idealistic commitment to the global protest movement that has arisen in opposition to the war in Iraq. Some historians sympathetic to Bush and Blair were busy rewriting the history of the First World War as a struggle between democracy and autocracy. The Germans were again being cast in the role of aggressive militarists, the carnage of the Somme being proclaimed 'a necessary sacrifice'. The bombing of Baghdad seemed to be spawning revisionist histories in which the Americans and the British were the eternal 'good guys'.

We at GWAG, by contrast, wanted an archaeology that connected with the spirit of protest, solidarity and humanity represented on the giant anti-war marches. We wanted to approach the First World War not from the perspective of any one of the belligerent nation-states, but from that of humanity as a whole. We see archaeology as a method of bringing people together, breaking down barriers, and seeking to understand a tragic past so that together we can work to make the world more peaceful.

GWAG's mission statement opens with this bitter comment made by Arundhati Roy, the Indian writer and anti-war activist in 2004: 'Flags are bits of coloured cloth that governments use first to shrink-wrap people's minds and then as ceremonial shrouds to bury the dead.' We were determined to include people of different nationalities. Nadia Durrani, for example, the other editor of this book, has a German mother, which impacts on her view of 'the enemy'. We also wanted people from disparate disciplines – from historians to engineers – and with different skills – including students, academics, detectorists, geophysicists, and excavators. This broad group is investigating how the modern world was created, why the recent past has been so bloody, and what lessons we should learn for the present.

Beyond this, archaeology still has the basic job of recovering new information from landscapes, excavations, and objects to help reveal the past. It is not the case that we know everything from maps, photographs, letters, diaries, memoirs, and war histories. Many of the details were never recorded. Leading First World War archaeologist Nick Saunders spells it out in his new book *Killing Fields*:

> … information retrieved by professional archaeologists is more accurate, more detailed and nuanced than that which can be gained only by looking at trench maps and aerial photographs in a more traditional military history approach. Archaeological fieldwork can identify sudden changes in the conditions of war, such as trench repairs made after heavy shelling, and the presence

of soldiers in a particular spot for a short period. Excavation can reveal unexpected structures, such as the entrance to a deep dugout or an ammunition depot, and the extent to which it may have changed hands between Allied and German forces.

As well as such technical details, there is archaeology's capacity to convey the raw human experience of war:

> Excavation also uncovers the terrible effects of industrialised war on human bodies, and the emotive artefacts belonging to or made by individuals. Such fine-grained details … can add new insights into the conduct and human cost of particular battles at specific locations … Archaeology can test assumptions and interpretations of military history, offer a soldier's-eye view of a skirmish or battle, and bring an intimacy to the experiences of soldiers through the objects they left behind.

The team at Theberton Hall Farm might hope to learn many things. No Zeppelins survive; there are only plans, photographs and fragments. No two Zeppelins were identical, and all were modified and repaired in service. Archaeology might reveal details of design, construction, and alteration. Bits of uniform and personal effects, on the other hand, might provide information about the crew, their experience of war, and how they coped with the discomforts, stresses and fears of combat. Fragments of weapons and the equipment carried might show discrepancies with the official record. Forensic analysis of the distribution and character of the debris might throw new light on the crash itself. The historical account might even need adjusting: while official records are often incomplete, eyewitness testimonies partial, and memories muddled, material evidence, while sometimes misinterpreted, cannot lie. Moreover, because you never know what you will find until you dig, it is axiomatic that archaeology often answers questions you had not even thought to ask: that is, it yields surprises and teaches unexpected lessons. Archaeologists dig partly to allow the evidence to tell them what it will.

Perhaps it is a lot of effort for the occasional tit-bit of fresh detail – a kind of micro-archaeology that loses significance as soon as we look up and see the whole vast canvas of the First World War. However, the power of such archaeology is not to be underestimated. Archaeology may be about the past but it always impacts the present – and this is perhaps especially true when you are dealing with what is sometimes called 'the recent past' or 'the contemporary past'. Let us say you dig a trench on the battlefield of the Somme today, empty it of ninety years' backfill, and restore its original size and shape. It is possible – if you are British, French, or German – that you are treading in the footsteps of a relative who had fought there, seen hell on earth there, perhaps even perished there. How will that make you feel? What will you think about war? What will you want to say to others? The archaeology of the First World War is the archaeology of our own recent ancestors. It throbs with memories, associations, and personal significances.

Fieldwork puts people into direct physical contact with an immediate and iconic past. Locations, structures, features and objects can trigger emotional responses which stimulate a deeper engagement with the past. People want to know more, but also find they have knowledge to contribute. Much information is locked up inside families and communities, or remains buried in archives and is yet to be researched. Fieldwork can act as a magnet which draws out memories, memorabilia, family history, and privately curated documents and artefacts. By kindling interest, engagement, and communication, fieldwork at a local site can be the dynamic core of a community's discovery of its own past.

When archaeologists re-expose the landscapes of 1914–18, when they reveal the physical context and material remains of the world's first modern industrialised war, allowing us a rare intimacy with those who fought it, they stir into motion a whirlpool of commemoration and controversy. Is this in fact archaeology, or is it at best voyeurism, at worst looting? Should the dead rest in peace, or should 'the missing' be recovered? Is this site of mud and blood, of twisted metal and shattered bone, a field of horror in a world gone mad, or a field of glory where heroes lie?

Julian's little team at Theberton Hall Farm were part of that enquiry. They had collected dozens of fragments of L48 detecting in the 25m-wide impact zone in the middle of Crofts Field. All were tiny. There were pieces of sheeting, fragments of girder, fabric grommets, rivet heads, and various melted and corroded lumps, all made from aluminium. A roughly equal number of objects were of copper, some nickel-plated, including tiny eyelets, fabric fasteners, and some electrical components. A handful of lead items appeared to derive from a radiator assembly.

Though the bits were so few and small that they would not have covered the base of a seed-tray (used traditionally by archaeologists for the recovery of on-site finds) they still caused a buzz. They were from L48, one of only five First World War Zeppelins shot down over Britain. They were testimony to a bizarre battle in the skies above that had been fought at the dawn of military aviation. For Julian Evan-Hart, veteran of numerous Second World War aviation crash digs, this was something special. No one had ever conducted an archaeological investigation of a Zeppelin crash site before. This was pioneering archaeology. Julian had found the exact spot in the landscape where L48 had come to earth, and now he held in the palm of his hand a corroded droplet of metal that had been formed ninety years before in the inferno of its destruction.

Though the popular image of metal-detectorists is that they are finding deeply buried hoards of treasure, in reality 90 per cent of finds come from cultivated land. Because most metal-detectors cannot pick up small

Fragments of L48. The uppermost object is a small section of geodetic (aluminium alloy) support structure (10cm x 2.5cm). Below, on the far left, is a key escutcheon plate (copper alloy), possibly from briefcase or map locker. To its right are small loops and eyelets (also copper alloy) from the outer fabric of the airship (about 8mm). Fragments of geodetic support structure were rare at this site. However, the example shown in this picture illustrates the remarkable condition of the aluminium alloy after ninety years in acidic coarse-sandy soil. The key escutcheon plate meant a lot to its finder, Julian Evan-Hart, who observed that this 'would have been used by a Zeppelin crewman over ninety years ago; it was incredible to hold in my hands something he would have touched.' (Julian Evan-Hart for GWAG)

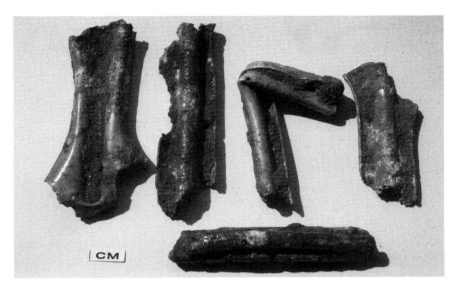

Five crumpled and twisted sections of aluminium-alloy geodetic support structure (average dimensions 11cm x 2.5cm). These fragments come from the very body of the airship and are the iconic structural elements. The destruction and stress are clearly apparent. These and all other Zeppelin fragments recovered from Crofts Field were found within about 10cm of the modern ground-surface. (Julian Evan-Hart for GWAG)

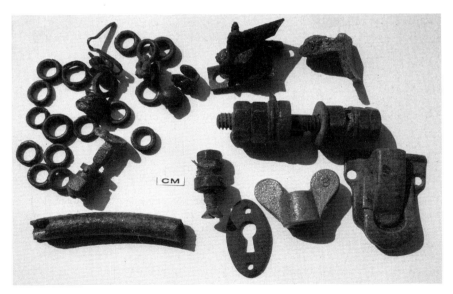

A selection of L48's eyelets, loops, fasteners, clips, screws, nuts/washers, and a wing nut marked '3' (plus the key escutcheon plate seen earlier). (Julian Evan-Hart for GWAG)

A selection of L48 aluminium-alloy airframe fragments. So intense was the heat that the aluminium alloy melted, forming molten droplets that can be seen on all of the items in this photograph. (Julian Evan-Hart for GWAG)

An officer's button made of copper alloy (with possible traces of silvering). Note the twisted rope and anchor emblem of the German Imperial Navy. Once again there is evidence of intense heat-subjection, represented by slight porosity of surface and blackened areas. Dimension: 19mm diameter. (Julian Evan-Hart for GWAG)

A possible officer's button backing-plate with the words *EXTRA FEIN* on the reverse (24mm in diameter). *Extra Fein* was a manufacturer's mark that appeared on numerous varieties of German transport buttons. 'Finds on crash-sites don't get much more personal than this,' said Julian Evan-Hart. 'My thoughts went out to the crew members, and I considered how they would have touched and fastened up their tunics with these very buttons just before setting off on their fateful flight.' (Julian Evan-Hart for GWAG)

A fired British 0.303 bullet. This bullet was probably fired at some height – the wind chill factor at extreme altitudes would have cooled down and shrunk the barrel of the guns, which in turn would have hugged the bullets far tighter than at ground level. When viewed close-up, these altitude 'hug-marks' are apparent on this copper-alloy bullet. Its location, depth, and the marks make it likely that this is one of the bullets that brought down L48. Dimensions: 37mm x 8mm. (Julian Evan-Hart for GWAG)

objects more than a few inches down, the vast bulk of these are from the heavily disturbed top-soil. That is why collections of metal-detected finds look so rough. They have been yanked from their original resting place by the deep-cutting, fast-moving blades of a motorised plough. Once in the plough-soil, they get this treatment on a regular basis. They also become more exposed to air and rain, and they get dowsed with highly corrosive chemical fertilisers. So modern agriculture is the single greatest destroyer of buried heritage. Metal artefacts in the plough-soil get battered and corroded to the point where they are unrecognisable. Metal-detectorists – provided their finds are fully recorded – should therefore be regarded as salvage archaeologists.

Julian's survey on Crofts Field was practical proof of this. Aluminium survives badly in the ground, and here were some of the tiny residual remains of L48 clearly fast degrading. Recovering this evidence now was a matter of rescuing it from total disintegration in the course of time.

There were two special finds, two diagnostic items that stood out when the little collection of non-descript bits and pieces of metal was spread out on the ground at the end of the search. One was a fired 0.303 bullet. This was the standard small-arms ammunition of British forces in the First World War. It was used in both the Lee Enfield short-magazine rifle and in the Lewis light machine-gun. The British night-fighters that had shot down L48 had been armed with Lewis machine-guns, and although this round was standard rather than specialised incendiary ammunition, it is possible – quite possible – that it is one of the rounds that brought down the airship. There is evidence that British pilots sometimes used a mix of standard, tracer and incendiary ammunition.

A simple bullet amid a scatter of metal bits: a faint ghostly shadow, perhaps, of that great aerial combat in the early hours of 17 June 1917. The team seemed to be touching both a Zeppelin and its destroyers. Zeppelins – like U-boats – were the infernal machines of a terrible new form of mechanised, industrialised, globalised warfare. The aerial bombing of cities and civilians has become central to our perceptions of war. Here were the remains of one of history's first strategic bombers. To engage with them, as Julian's team had done, was to engage with a powerful cultural nexus of ideas, images and associations that is part of modern human identity and political consciousness.

The other special find was more poignant still. It was a battered copper button from the tunic of one of the airship's crew, possibly that of an officer, engraved with the manufacturer's marking *EXTRA FEIN*. No one had touched this button in the ninrty years since its owner had perished with L48. The war was suddenly very close, very intimate, very real.

The crew of L48 were neither 'heroes' nor 'baby-killers'. They were ordinary men who, because of the age in which they lived, were required to do extraordinary things. And because the age was one of madness, some of the things they did were monstrous: like dropping bombs on sleeping children. They did these things because they were ordered to, thinking it their duty to obey such orders, and perhaps, if any had doubts, fearing the consequences if they refused. They did no more or less than millions of other ordinary men sucked into the vortex of violence – some, no doubt, also lured into it by nationalism, the promise of heroism, even the romance of war. Yet in retrospect, blame does not attach to the common people who were dragooned onto the killing fields of the Great War. The rulers of the world had created the crisis and the carnage. The men of L48 were victims of war no less than those they tried to bomb. They died horrible deaths, a small group of terrified men clinging to burning wreckage as it fell from the sky, turning to pulp as they hit the ground if they jumped, roasting to death in a prison of melting metal if they did not.

Ninety years on, Julian Evan-Hart was standing in the field where they died, holding a button from one of the dead men's tunics. He had found where to dig. He had completed his mission. But he was left with a tangle of raw emotions.

3
Weapons of Mass Destruction

On 13 June 1917, a German bomb went through the roof of the London County Council School in Upper North Street, Poplar, dropping through two storeys, and exploding in an infant classroom. Eighteen five year olds were killed and a further thirty-seven people injured. Jack Brown was in the next classroom. Interviewed in 2006 for a BBC2 *Timewatch* documentary, *The First Blitz*, his recollections were vivid.

I think the bombs fell somewhere around 11 o'clock in the morning, if I remember rightly. Our teacher said, 'Oh, well, let's have some air raid drill, which consisted of pulling down the flap of the desk and getting underneath, which we did, and of course, we'd no sooner got underneath than all the glass and everything fell in, and there was smoke and fumes and all sorts of things around the place.

It's all silent in my memory. I don't remember a bang as such. Whether the bang deafened me or what, I don't know. Even when I remember the glass all coming in and smashing down all over the place, I still don't associate sound with it.

What I remember, there was no panic, no fear, because it was so new, so sudden and everything that the children were just bewildered, I think, and stunned. So then we walked out into the playground. While I was standing there, the caretaker came out with the first of the bodies.

Then afterwards, when I got home, my mother came tearing down the street, with one shoe on, and the other one in her hand. Always remember her now, tearing down, and course, I don't know, she just stopped and looked at me. What happened after that I don't remember.

Well, the next morning we went back to the school again, and when we got there, Mr Denner, the headmaster, was there with the school register, and he stood there reading the names out from the register, and I remember that as he stood there and the names came out, he was crying.

It was one of the worst incidents in the German strategic bombing campaign of 1914–18. This was a new and terrible kind of war: the first time in history that civilians on the 'home front' had been deliberately targeted by aerial bombing. Though it had been predicted before the war, the moral shock when it came was extreme. The popular press denounced the 'Huns' and 'baby-killers', and ran pictures of women and children killed in the raids. The funerals of victims became public events. That of the dead children of Upper North Street School was one of the biggest in the history of the East End. There were anti-German riots in some cities, and shops whose owners had German-sounding names were targeted. Men in Royal Flying Corps uniform were sometimes abused in the streets for their failure to stop the bombers getting through. These were the overt expressions of deep-rooted and widespread fear. Thousands spent sleepless nights, sobbing and trembling, expecting bombs to fall at any moment, even when no raid was in progress. Tens of thousands crowded into basements and underground stations.

Upper North Street School had been bombed by a Gotha, a conventional aircraft, but until May 1917, except for some minor coastal raids, the strategic bombing campaign had been mounted exclusively by Zeppelin airships. These huge, sinister shapes, humming slowly through the night skies over British cities, emblazoned with the black cross of Imperial Germany, were the new terror weapons of the industrial age. Though some in the German High Command had remained resolutely sceptical about their military potential, others, with the enthusiastic backing of nationalist public opinion, had vested great hopes in the Zeppelins. None more so than the man whose brainchild they were, the Württemberg aristocrat and former army officer Count Graf Ferdinand von Zeppelin. After forced retirement from the army in 1890, Zeppelin's fierce nationalism had been re-channelled into developing airship technology. He had devoted himself and his fortune to ensuring that the Fatherland was not outstripped in the air. Aristocratic patriotism fused with bourgeois science to produce an infernal machine that symbolised the new Imperial Germany. When the first airship flew in July 1900,

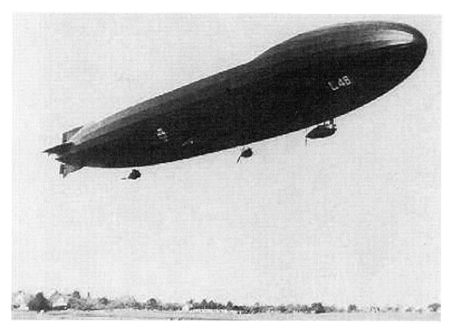

An attractive souvenir-like shot of Zeppelin L48 in flight. Yet the writing was on the wall, and soon the L48 would lie wrecked in a field in the corner of East Anglia.

Zeppelin became a hero of the nationalist camp. When later a succession of abortive models exhausted his private resources, the project was kept afloat by a mixture of venture capital, state grants, and a public lottery. By the outbreak of war, a fleet of airships was offering commercial flights, and both army and navy had purchased airships for long-range recon-naissance. But many, including Zeppelin, conceived a more sinister role for the airship in war: that of strategic bomber. The virility of the nation was to find its measure in a Science Age killing-machine.

It had long been predicted. British science-fiction writer H.G. Wells, in a series of magazine articles published in 1901, imagined a future battle for air supremacy being fought out in the skies above the great centres of industrial civilisation:

> The victor in that aerial struggle will tower with pitilessly watchful eyes over his adversary, will concentrate his guns and all his strength unobserved, will mark all his adversary's roads and communications and sweep them with

sudden, incredible disasters of shot and shell. The moral effect of this predominance will be enormous.

A few years later, he turned this apocalyptic vision into the popular novel *The War in the Air* (1908), in which a fleet of German airships bombs its way down New York's Broadway, engulfing Manhattan in flames, executing 'one of the most cold-blooded slaughters in the world's history, in which men who were neither excited nor, except for the remotest chance of a bullet, in any danger, poured death and destruction upon homes and crowds below.'

Wells had imitators. The airship became a staple of pulp fiction. The popular press carried images of cities in flames beneath hovering grey giants. Politicians debated whether Britain was imperilled by sinister new weapons of mass destruction. Wells himself – no pacifist despite his Fabian socialist politics – joined with other notables in urging the British government to prioritise air defence. Popular fears were fed by German propagandists for whom the Zeppelin was a wonder-weapon capable of leaping the Channel barrier which otherwise rendered Britain an invulnerable island-fortress. Little wonder that when war broke out the authorities were inundated with imagined sightings of German raiders. It was even rumoured that a Zeppelin was hiding in the Lake District and coming out at night to reconnoitre. But, in fact, for a time, there were no raids at all.

There were many reasons that the Zeppelins did not come. At first, the war of movement had seemed to promise rapid victory; only when trench stalemate had set in, and the British blockade begun to bite, did the advocates of strategic bombing gain a hearing. Still the means were lacking. The army had begun the war with ten airships, the navy with only one, and this meagre force was soon depleted by operational losses in Belgium and France. The Zeppelin force was further battered by pre-emptive strikes. Winston Churchill, who as First Lord of the Admiralty had responsibility for home defence, was unable to offer any: he had a grand total of thirty-three anti-aircraft guns, twenty-eight of which were completely useless 1pdr 'pom-poms'. His characteristically aggressive response was to order the Royal Naval Air Service to launch a series of daring raids against the Zeppelin bases on the Continent. Coming in low to drop tiny bombs, the British naval pilots destroyed a Zeppelin in its shed at Düsseldorf on 8 October, then a second at Friedrichshaven on 21 November.

A third barrier to Zeppelin raiding was lack of political will. The bombing of cities and civilians violated military honour and the rules of

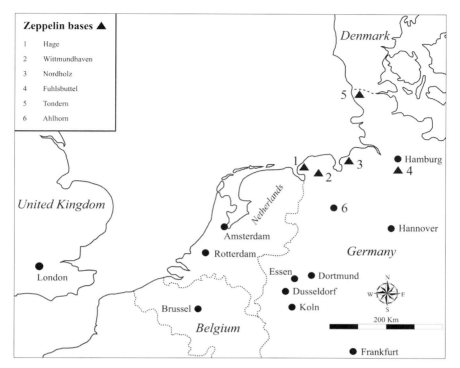

Zeppelin bases ▲

1	Hage
2	Wittmundhaven
3	Nordholz
4	Fuhlsbuttel
5	Tondern
6	Ahlhorn

Map showing the theatre of operations during the First Blitz. The Zeppelins usually crossed directly over the North Sea from their North German bases, making landfall on the East Anglian coast, then commonly turned south-west to attack London. (Dave Hibbitt for GWAG)

war, representing an awesome escalation of conflict likely to induce retaliation. The Kaiser, in particular, was squeamish. He refused to authorise any air raids on Britain until 10 January 1915, and unrestricted aerial bombing was not permitted until 20 July. What drove the change was the inexorable logic of total war. When the war of movement ended in October 1914, a war of attrition had begun, one in which industrial output and civilian morale counted as much as the outcome of great battles. This was a war which found the Central Powers disadvantaged. Already, war casualties had cut a swathe through the German working and middle classes, while the British naval blockade was damaging industry and starving families. Unable to break the stalemate and threatened with slow strangulation, Germany's leaders turned to the magicians of the wonder-weapons.

These pages: German bombing during the First World War was relatively ineffective, but there were occasional successes, as when Kew Waterworks was hit by Gotha bombers early in 1918. A series of vivid images recorded the effects. Though industry and infrastructure were specifically targeted, the aim was also to terrorise the civilian population. The novelty of aerial bombing and the vividness of news reports gave rise

to exaggerated fears, widespread panic, and a major problem of absenteeism and lost production in war industries. It was this popular reaction to the bombing that constituted its greatest effect, forcing the authorities to divert resources into home defence. (Courtesy of Thames Water)

Supreme among them was Peter Strasser, commander of the Naval Airship Division, one of the great pioneers of military aviation. Austere and aloof, possessed of steely determination and efficiency, he was wholly dedicated to the service, deeply concerned with the welfare of his men, and unflinching in his belief in the power and potential of the airship. On 10 August 1916 he wrote to his superiors:

> The performance of the big airships has reinforced my conviction that England can be overcome by means of airships, inasmuch as the country will be deprived of the means of existence through increasingly extensive destruction of cities, factory complexes, dockyards, harbour works with war and merchant ships lying therein, railways, etc. ... airships offer a certain means of victoriously ending the war.

Some allowed themselves to be convinced. Others reflected that, if nothing else, it would be good for morale. Certainly, the German press, in a series of sensational reports, toasted the heroism of the aircrew and their apparent triumphs. They were the Fatherland's avenging furies. On one raid, aircrew dropped a bag on a small parachute. Inside was a scraped ham-bone. The shank was painted on one side with the German tricolour and the message 'A memento from starved-out Germany', and on the other with a cartoon depicting a Zeppelin dropping a bomb on the head of British Foreign Secretary Sir Edward Grey.

In fact, achievement fell well short of Strasser's promises. In a total of fifty-three airship raids between January 1915 and August 1918, during which almost 6,000 bombs were dropped, total casualties were just 1,900, and total damage estimated at around £1.5 million (about a quarter of what Britain was spending *each day* on the war). The problems were numerous. Zeppelins were operationally dependent on good weather, clear skies, favourable winds, and the darkness of long, moonless nights: ideal 'Zepp nights' were few. Aerial navigation was in its infancy and relied on a haphazard mix of dead reckoning, radio signals, and direct observation of the ground below. Airship captains rarely knew their location with any accuracy, and sometimes could be a hundred miles out. Even if they found their way, targets were hard to identify, bomb-sights were crude, and it was pure chance if a bomb struck any sort of military installation. Carpet bombing – an obvious alternative to precision bombing – was entirely precluded by the small numbers of airships available and their modest bomb-loads. Operational analysis to identify errors and improve efficiency was frustrated by British censorship; the often hopelessly optimistic claims of airship captains provided the only information about the effects of air raids.

The British faced a heavy political cost. Zeppelins were terror weapons with an impact out of all proportion to the damage done. On the night of 8–9 September 1915, airship ace Heinrich Mathy's L13 had cut a swathe across London, starting massive fires in the clothing warehouses north of St Paul's, and scoring direct hits on two packed motor-buses near Liverpool Street Station. The result was half a million pounds' damage – a third of the total inflicted by the Zeppelins in the entire war – and well over a hundred casualties, including fifteen people killed outright on the two buses. Just over a month later, on 13–14 October, another Zeppelin, Joachim Breithaupt's L15, reached the heart of the capital and dropped a string of bombs on the West End's theatres and Inns of Courts. The second bomb exploded in a street, ruptured a gas main, and ignited the stream of escaping gas. The street and nearby bars and theatres had been crowded. Amid millions of sherds of glass, seventeen lay dead and a further twenty-one wounded. One woman had been blown to pieces, another cut in half by a sheet of glass. Altogether that night, seventy-one people were killed and 128 wounded, making it the bloodiest Zeppelin raid of the war.

Again and again, the raiders got clean away. A storm of protest broke around the government and military authorities. The press raged about 'murder by Zeppelin' and the absence of effective defence. Politicians addressed packed meetings. There were angry exchanges in the House of Commons. Admiral Sir Percy Scott, a renowned naval gunnery expert, was put in charge of London's anti-aircraft batteries. General Sir David Henderson, commander of the Royal Flying Corps, in a frosty personal interview with Secretary for War Kitchener, was ordered to commit his fighters against the Zeppelins. Britain, with its established industrial economy, had grown technologically conservative and failed to embrace military aviation. Now it was paying the price. Now it had to catch up fast. Coming from behind, it had to wage a battle for air supremacy with enemy raiders who were already in the skies above its capital.

Air power always depends mainly on technology. It could not be otherwise, for powered flight, and therefore aerial warfare, was an invention of the industrial age. The Germans continued to innovate, developing new generations of more powerful Zeppelins – able to climb higher,

Above and below: A short letter written on the back of a photographic card depicting Councillor John Nisbet and his wife, residents of South London, gives an impression of the impact of the bombing on ordinary people.

On the back of the card John Nisbet writes: 'This photo was taken a few days before coming here by Mr Osker. We went over there to tea, Mrs Osker suggested we should be taken in, it was done in a hurry at a small table – By the way London was badly hit by the Zeppelins on two nights last week, 12 were killed in Canterbury Road Old Kent Road on the first night and on the second the destruction in Wood Street City amounted to two million pounds. On this same night a Zep visited our neighbourhood and was driven off by the guns on One Tree Hill. We were woken out of our sleep at 12 o/c and had a most interesting time – the neighbourhood was quite alive all being up.' (Courtesy of Steve Grindlay)

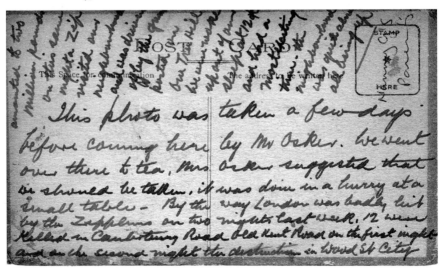

beyond the range of defending guns and planes, yet carrying heavier bomb-loads. The British began the race from a standing start: thirty-three guns to defend the whole of Britain, most of them useless. Even with the pressure on and some resources available, there was still the question of what exactly to do: were guns or planes the solution? At first, guns were favoured, and only slowly did the number of fighters dedicated to home defence build.

It seems obvious now. Guns can defend fixed positions, but they are necessarily static, or relatively so (since even guns mounted on trucks, as many were, could not actually pursue the raiders). Only aeroplanes could engage in a battle for air supremacy by hunting and destroying airships. The problem was that at first the fighters achieved very little, so their potential remained hidden. Lack of lights and guns allowed the raiders to range widely. They were hard to locate in cloud and haze, and their altitude ceiling and rate of climb were greater (and increasingly so as new models were introduced) than their opponents'. The fighters were too few, and, even when lucky enough to locate and close with an airship, lacked an effective weapon system. Only in the autumn of 1916 did the British home defence achieve the critical mass necessary to tip the balance against the raiders: an early warning system to alert the defenders; a ring of lights and guns that kept the attackers corralled in a killing zone around the capital; and a sufficient number of fighters to patrol this zone, manned by pilots trained in night-flying, committed to hunter-killer tactics, and deploying new explosive and incendiary ammunition.

The Germans knew the British defences were thickening. They had developed a new generation of Zeppelins – the 'Thirties' series – that was intended to render these defences obsolete. They did not. The dramatic climax was the shooting down of Heinrich Mathy's L31 on 1–2 October 1916: the incontrovertible proof that the Zeppelins could no longer attack the London defences and expect to survive.

Mathy, a veteran of numerous raids, was a master navigator and aerial tactician, with an unrivalled reputation among airship captains for cool determination and daring. Nonetheless, when he set out with ten other airships from their North German bases on the afternoon of 1 October, the old confidence was no longer there. He was now the sole survivor among a core group of veteran commanders in a highly specialised service. The tight-knit military elite of which he was the leading representative had recently been shaken by heavy losses.

An archive photograph of a First World War anti-aircraft gun on Pole Hill overlooking the Lea Valley in Essex. Note the ammunition crates stacked nearby. With London-sprawl suburban housing in the background, the photograph conveys the way in which the entire landscape was militarised by the impact of the air war.

When history's first strategic bombing campaign had begun early in 1915, the giant airships had come and gone with impunity. Later, there had been occasional losses to accidents and enemy fire. Then, suddenly, just a week before, on the night of 23–24 September, two of the new super-Zeppelins had been shot down. One of them had turned into a raging fireball which plunged to earth killing all on board. The horror had been visible to the rest of the airship fleet strung out across the skies over southern Britain. The event had shattered the nerves of the German airship crews, and many were showing signs of combat fatigue. Among Mathy's crew, the mess-room mood was sombre. There was much talk of the losses. Men slept uneasily, haunted by bad dreams and visions of falling airships. Even Mathy was on edge. Though he endeavoured to behave as normal, his men noticed the change: his appearance more serious, his features more sharply and deeply graven in his face. And in the privacy of his quarters, he confessed his fears in a letter to his young wife, at home nursing a new baby:

Peterson is dead, Böcker a prisoner. Hertha, the war is becoming a serious matter. ... During these days, when you lay our little daughter down to sleep, a good angel will see you and will read what is in your heart, and he will hasten to guard my ship against the dangers which throng the air everywhere about her.

But a week later, he was dead.

Airship crew knew they took risks. The wartime casualty rate was 40 per cent. And 2½ miles up, there were special terrors not faced by men on the ground. There was nowhere to run to, no way of escape; one lived or died as the machine flew or crashed. Men perished in the airships because engines failed, or storms blew up, or commanders simply lost their way and ran out of fuel. On the morning of 2 February 1916, the crew of L19 were seen clinging to the wreckage of their airship by a British trawler captain 110 miles east of the Yorkshire coast. He refused to rescue them, fearful they might seize his vessel, and they were left to be consumed by the cold wastes of the North Sea. Six months later, a message in a bottle washed up on the Swedish coast was found to contain the German commander's last official report. Above all, airship crew feared being set on fire, either in the air or trapped in a tangle of flaming wreckage on the ground. In the mess-rooms, they debated whether or not, if their airship was shot down, to jump at the last minute. The impact of those who did sometimes left macabre imprints in the ground.

The defences around London – searchlights, anti-aircraft guns, and home-defence fighter squadrons – had thickened alarmingly. Individually, neither guns nor planes were a serious threat. It was estimated after the war that only one in 8,000 of the anti-aircraft shells fired scored a hit, and that around 90 per cent of home-defence pilots never so much as saw their enemy. But *en masse*, a network of lights, guns and planes, if sufficiently dense, could create a zone of lethal danger over the British capital. By the early autumn of 1916, such a system was in place. Rings of lights and guns were activated without hesitation and at long range. Once enemy raiders were spotted, they were liable, on a clear night, to be held in a pyramid of light-rays and targeted by numerous 3in quick-firing anti-aircraft guns, some in fixed positions, others moved around on lorries. Firing fifteen rounds a minute to a maximum vertical range of 18,000ft, the guns were able to fill the sky with enough bursting

An archive photograph taken in 1915 of the Royal Naval Air Service Airfield at Chingford in Essex. This was the photograph unearthed by GWAG's industrial historian Jim Lewis, and test-pitting on the site has relocated some of the buildings shown in the background. Various aircraft are depicted in the foreground – a Grahame-White 'box-kite', a Maurice Farman 'Shorthorn', an Avro 504K, a BE2c, and a Bristol 'Bullet'.

shrapnel to keep the raiders hovering on the fringes of the capital – the killing zone of the British fighters.

The staple of the home-defence squadrons was the BE2c biplane. Its main advantage was exceptional stability, which made it especially suitable for the hazardous landings of night-flying missions, as well as constituting an excellent firing platform in the sky. But it was painfully slow: maximum speed was under 75mph, and it took more than half an hour to climb to its ceiling of 10,000ft. There was, therefore, only one effective way to operate. At each station, the on-duty pilot would wait by his machine for an air-raid warning and the order to scramble. He would then ascend onto a regular patrol line for his three-hour stint in the air. If, however, he sighted an enemy raider, his standing orders were to pursue and attack. The air-war policy of the British was to gain supremacy by relentlessly locating and destroying all enemy aircraft. The British fighters were out to hunt and kill. The handful of young officer-pilots

The FE2b fighter aircraft flown from Orfordness Airfield by Second Lieutenant Frank Holder and Sergeant Sydney Ashby against Zeppelin L48 in the early hours of 17 June 1917. It is a two-seater, with the engine and propeller behind the pilot, so that it was 'pushed' rather than 'pulled' through the air. Its main armament was a forward-mounted 0.303 Lewis light machine-gun on a swivel that was operated by the gunner (Ashby) stationed in the forward cockpit, but a second gun could be operated by the pilot (Holder) sitting behind. (Orfordness via Ray Rimell)

who flew them – rising alone in open cockpits into the freezing night air – formed the deadly cutting-edge of a home-defence system that now employed 17,000 men. As the Zeppelins hummed towards Britain, remote listening stations picked up their radio messages, and patrol ships and coastal observation-posts watched for them in the sky. Early warnings were phoned to Room 40 at the Admiralty in London, and from there the message went out 'Take air raid action'. Lights snapped on, guns were made ready, and aircraft at a dozen airfields coughed into life and were sent bumping across the grass for take-off.

Despite the danger, Heinrich Mathy in L31 remained determined to penetrate the defences and bomb the enemy capital on the night of 1–2 October 1916. After making landfall near Lowestoft at 9.00p.m., he headed south-west for London. But the threat of converging searchlights caused him to sheer away northwards again at around 10.45p.m. Only now were the home-defence pilots getting onto their patrol lines.

Mathy circled for a time, then throttled his engines and attempted to cross the northern gun defences by drifting silently with the wind, hoping to remain undetected. But when he reopened his engines at 12.30a. m., lights and guns burst into life, and the commotion attracted the attention of the fighters, now prowling for prey along the furthest edges of the capital. Second Lieutenant Wulfstan Tempest saw a small cigar-shaped object illuminated by a pyramid of seachlights and bracketed by exploding shrapnel: Mathy's Zeppelin. As the BE2c fighter raced towards it, L31 turned sharply away, jettisoned its bombs, and began climbing steeply.

Mathy was not fast enough. Though forced to hand-operate a broken fuel-pump, Tempest closed the gap and dived on the rising airship. He fired first as he dived, then again as he flew beneath the monster. No effect. He next banked his plane and came in once more beneath the tail. Flying under the airship's hull, he opened fire for the third time, raking the length of it with bullets. At first he despaired when again nothing seemed to happen, and then 'I saw her begin to go red inside like an enormous Chinese lantern.'

The BE12 fighter aircraft. A plane of this type was flown from Goldhanger Airfield by Second Lieutenant 'Don' Watkins against Zeppelin L48 in the early hours of 17 June 1917. It is a conventional single-seater, with the engine and propeller forward of the pilot/ gunner's cockpit. (P.L. Gray via Ray Rimell)

That autumn, the British pilots deployed a new weapon. No longer dependent on dropping bombs or explosive darts over the side, nor on the standard machine-gun ammunition that appeared to have no effect whatever on the giant gas-bags, the home-defence squadrons now filled their ammunition belts with a mixture of tracer and newly designed explosive and incendiary bullets. The idea was to blow a hole in the fabric of an airship and then ignite the escaping hydrogen as it mixed with air. The new weapon had claimed three airships in a month. Now it claimed a fourth.

Mathy's Zeppelin shot 200ft upwards, hung in the air for a moment, and then began to fall. Gas cells exploded into incandescent fireballs. Sheets of envelope-fabric were ripped off and blasted into the night sky. Flames streaked up the sides and the airship became an immense torch, glowing orange, yellow and white, hissing and roaring as it plunged earthwards.

Tempest only narrowly escaped the inferno. He was forced to nose-dive, put his machine into a spin, and corkscrew his way clear. It left him feeling sick and disoriented. When he eventually picked out the night flares of an airfield runway, he misjudged his height in the fog and crashed, losing his undercarriage and clunking his head on the butt of his Lewis gun. He was lucky to suffer nothing worse than a cut and a headache; landing crashes accounted for most of the twenty-eight fighter pilots killed in the air war over Britain.

The remains of L31 landed in a field at Potters Bar, about 10 miles north of London. All the crew were killed, most of them burnt in the wreckage, though one had jumped and was found half embedded in the soil, apparently still breathing when first seen: the German airship ace himself.

The disaster had been witnessed across London the night before. Spontaneous cheering and applause had filled the streets. Now huge crowds gathered at the wreck site to bear witness to the British victory. Three of the new super-Zeppelins, each commanded by a veteran captain, had been shot down. It was the turning point in the air war: the British had defeated the world's first strategic bombing campaign. The morale of the German airship crew was shattered. One, commenting on Mathy's death, said, 'It was the aeroplane firing the incendiary bullet that brought about his downfall, and with him the life and soul of our airship service went out too.'

A DH2 fighter aircraft in flight at Orfordness. A plane of this type was flown by Flight Commander Henry Saundby against Zeppelin L48 in the early hours of 17 June 1917. As a 'pusher' biplane, with engine and propeller behind the cockpit, it had the bug-like appearance of the FE2b, but it was much smaller, being a single-seater, and its performance was better. (Orfordness via Ray Rimell)

Though German airship enthusiasts like Strasser refused to concede defeat, the number of raids fell off sharply. Whereas between January 1915 and October 1916 there had been forty-one airship attacks, between then and the end of the war there were just twelve. The later raids, moreover, were of little effect. The strength of British defences drove the Germans to expedients that condemned the Zeppelins to futility: the new generation of 'height-climbers' – like L48 – could rise beyond the reach of enemy guns and fighters, but only by exposing themselves to the unexplored hazards of the sub-stratosphere, and operating at heights that made accurate navigation and targeting quite impossible. The average damage inflicted by a raider slumped from around £6,500 before 1–2 October 1916 to less than £2,000 afterwards. And, despite safety from enemy fire in the sub-stratosphere, losses continued to mount.

During the 'silent raid' of 19–20 October 1917 – silent because the raiders mostly passed unseen and unheard – five of the eleven airships that set out were lost to the gale that raged across France during their return journey. Often, anyway, conditions aloft were such that airships preferred the risk of descending into the range of the British fighters. In the final Zeppelin raid of the war, on 5–6 August 1918, L70, the newest and most powerful of German airships, was shot down in flames by a British fighter off the Norfolk coast. All hands were lost. Among them was Peter Strasser himself. His death marked the end of the airship as a strategic bomber. 'We were overcome with grief,' recalled one of Strasser's few surviving veteran captains after the war. 'There was not one among us … who did not feel that Strasser's death left a yawning gulf that nothing could fill. We no longer took the same interest in flying; for the spark which Peter had kindled in our breasts had been extinguished.'

Morale and discipline collapsed at the end of October 1918. Zeppelin ground-crew joined the German Revolution, arrested their officers, and took control of the air-bases. Many of the elite flight crew – long-term military professionals – remained loyal to the old regime, however, and it was a group of them who, on the morning of 23 June 1919, entered the Zeppelin sheds, removed the shores beneath the suspended hulls, slacked off the suspension cables, and allowed the machines to fall and smash beyond repair on the concrete floors below. 'We didn't want them falling into the hands of those damned Communists in Berlin,' explained one of the conspirators afterwards. The first strategic bombing force in history had been scuttled by counter-revolutionaries.

Long before, however, in the skies over Britain, the aeroplane bomber had rendered the airship obsolete. Though there had been occasional German aeroplane raids across the Channel from late 1914 onwards, lack of range had limited these to pinprick attacks on coastal towns. But the Germans had in the meantime been developing a heavy bomber – the Gotha – and by late spring 1917 this had been perfected, mass produced, and formed into a new 'England Squadron'. British Intelligence had been poor and the first mass raid – in daylight on 25 May 1917 by twenty-three bombers – came as a shock.

The Gotha was a large, twin-engine bomber, with a maximum speed of 80mph, maximum ceiling of 15,000ft, and, crucially, maximum range of 500 miles. Each was manned by three men – a commander-navigator (and bomber), a pilot, and a rear-gunner – and, in addition to the bombs, there was a defensive armament of three machine-guns. Flying in a tight V-shaped formation for mutual support, the Gothas' combined firepower made them highly dangerous to fighters. Even when they lost formation and could be tackled individually, they remained dangerous to approach, deploying a forward machine-gun and two at the rear, one directed upwards, the other designed to shoot downwards through an opening in the base of the fuselage, covering the combat aeroplane's traditional blind-spot. Consequently, more Gothas were lost in crash-landings than to hostile action.

On 28 September 1917, yet another new weapon entered the fray: the Giant. Powered by six engines, these aircraft were twice the size of a Gotha and carried four times its bomb-load; they were bigger, in fact, than any German bomber of the Second World War. Manned by up to nine men and defended by between four and seven machine-guns, they were able to fight off veritable swarms of fighters, and none was ever shot down. Fortunately for the British, research and development was ongoing, the design was never standardised, and relatively few were actually built. The staple bomber remained the Gotha.

By the autumn of 1917, however, the Germans were sometimes losing as many as five bombers in a raid to a combination of anti-aircraft fire, fighter attack, and crash-landings. The cost of both investment in the research and development of new designs and in the mass production necessary to replace operational losses was too much for a German economy beginning to buckle under the strains of total war. The strategic bombing campaign was largely given up during the great offensives on the Western Front in spring and autumn 1918.

The British, in any case, were beginning to threaten serious retaliation. By the end of the war, they had more than 250 twin-engine Handley Page heavy bombers in service, some of them mounting night raids on the industrial cities of the Saar and Ruhr. At the Armistice, they had also taken delivery of the first of a new class of four-engine Handley Page bomber, a machine with four times the bomb-load of its predecessor, and the range to reach Berlin: a British plane which finally – too late to be used – matched the capabilities of its German counterparts. Just before the end, deploying its greater industrial power, the Entente was poised to win the aerial bombing war.

The effects of the campaign had been considerable. Total casualties in the German air offensive against Britain in the First World War were only about 1,400 killed and 3,500 wounded, with total damage valued at around £3 million (about half a day's British war expenditure). Yet the blackouts, shutdowns and absenteeism directly attributable to the raids had a huge (though incalculable) impact on war production, and the diversion of military resources to home defence amounted to 17,000 men, 470 guns, 620 searchlights, and 380 aeroplanes. More than this, the strategic bomber was a terror weapon. The results on the ground could be horrific. On 13 June 1917, Siegfried Sassoon, on convalescent leave at home, was witness to the effects of a Gotha bomb hitting a train waiting to depart Liverpool Street Station. Horrified people were hurrying from the scene. The corpse of an old man was pushed past on a luggage trolley. The experience of the trenches seemed no sort of preparation. Here was ordinary life suddenly reduced to blood, twisted metal, and shattered glass.

> … one was helpless; an invisible enemy sent destruction spinning down from a fine weather sky; poor old men bought a railway ticket and were trundled away again dead on a barrow; wounded women lay about the station groaning.

Sassoon was witness to the raid which also destroyed the infant class at Upper North Street School.

THE MEN WHO BROUGHT DOWN ZEPPELIN L48

Left: Second Lieutenant Frank Holder. (Orfordness via Ray Rimell)

Below: Second Lieutenant 'Don' Watkins (left) with other members of 50 Home Defence Squadron. The aeroplane behind them is a BE2c, the most successful British night-fighter of the First Blitz. (D. Whetton via Ray Rimell)

Flight Commander Henry Saundby. (Lady Saundby via Ray Rimell)

On 28–29 January 1918, a Giant dropped a huge bomb outside a print-works in Covent Garden, where some 500 people were sheltering in the basement. The blast caused part of the building to collapse and the rest to catch fire. Two of the three basement exits were blocked. One woman's baby was blown out of her arms and never seen again. It was among thirty-eight killed and eighty-five wounded in the disaster. The screams of those trapped beneath the rubble of burning buildings would haunt those who heard them ever after. Little wonder that thousands flocked to tube stations, basements and other refuges during raids. At the height of the Gotha attacks on the capital, in September and October 1917, at least 100,000 Londoners were sheltering in the tube. Little wonder, too, that men at the front, hearing of the raids in letters from home, began to fear for the safety of their families. 'You know, dear, it's hard to be out here fighting and yet your wife and children can't be safe,' wrote Private John Mudd to his wife Lizzie.

War had once been a matter of small professional armies fighting distant colonial campaigns. Now mass citizen-armies fought one another in Europe itself. But the German air offensive against Britain showed that war had changed in another respect. The brave warriors holding the line were no longer an effective defence of homes and families. The infernal machines of industrialised warfare could transcend the two-dimensional war of fronts to rain death from the skies on cities and civilians. The advocates of strategic bombing usually maintained that their targets were military and industrial – power plants, steel mills, munitions factories, dockyards – and that their purpose was to cripple the enemy war effort. Aircrew preferred to believe that their targets were armed men, not women and children. Even a man as ruthless as Strasser had felt bound to return home without releasing bombs after failing to locate a military target. Yet this model military professional also spoke of 'the dread of the airships prevailing in wide strata of society'. His superior, Rear Admiral Paul Behncke, deputy chief of the naval staff, was more explicit: air raids, he wrote in an enthusiastic memorandum as early as 20 August 1914:

> may be expected ... to cause panic in the population which may possibly render it doubtful that the war can be continued. ... In general, air attacks with aeroplanes and airships ... promise considerable material and moral results. They must therefore be considered an effective means of damaging England.

Men like Strasser and Behncke knew that civilians were bound to die when they targeted military and industrial installations close to residential districts. But when they talked of 'the dread of airships', 'panic in the population', 'material *and moral* results', they implied something more: that civilians were actually targets, and that Zeppelins, Gothas and Giants were terror weapons designed to break the enemy population's will to resist.

Inter-war advocates of strategic bombing – men shaped by the experience of the First World War – were in no doubt that civilians were targets. Rebellious colonial subjects could be terrorised into submission at minimal cost by bombs rained on them from the sky. Urban workers – their role central in industrialised wars of *matériel* – might be driven to flight or revolt by saturation bombing of residential districts. The promise of the strategic bombers was that they could drive the price of resistance too high for the enemy to bear. To their political masters they offered a cut-price technological fix. A new and terrible kind of war had been pioneered in the skies over London in 1915. In the century to follow it would consume millions.

4

'Take Air-Raid Action': the Early Warning System

Jim Lewis and Chris Mackie were on the cliffs at Hunstanton in the summer of 2005. Though only about 20m above the sea, the cliffs are high by Norfolk standards, and visually spectacular, with bands of white chalk, red chalk, and brown carstone. Looking west across The Wash, you can see the pencil-line of Lincolnshire stretching along the horizon. Looking north, you stare out into the grey wastes of the North Sea. There is a ruined medieval chapel just back from the cliff, a whitewashed Victorian lighthouse of 1840 near the edge, and a century-old red-brick coastguard tower a little further along, with a row of coastguard cottages behind. The lighthouse, the coastguard tower, and the coastguard cottages are today private residences. In summer the Hunstanton cliffs offer seaside tourist facilities like pitch and putt, donkey rides, and ice-cream sales. Ninety years ago, they were the front-line of an invisible technological war to defend Britain against aerial bombardment.

Jim and Chris had come in search of a Marconi wireless direction-finding station from the First World War. Apart from a three-year spell in the RAF servicing wireless communications equipment, Jim had spent most of his career working in the consumer electronics industry, latterly for Thorn EMI Ferguson in the Lea Valley, north-east London. Now retired, he continues to work as an industrial historian. His particular expertise is the small-arms industry in the Lea Valley. But he is also a member of the Great War Archaeology Group, and he was on Hunstanton cliffs as part of the group's search for the Zeppelin War.

Chris Mackie was there to help. A retired National Trust property manager, Chris is also an experienced amateur archaeologist, with detailed

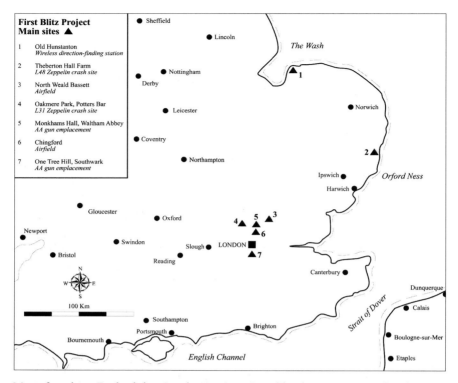

**First Blitz Project
Main sites ▲**

1   Old Hunstanton
     Wireless direction-finding station

2   Theberton Hall Farm
     L48 Zeppelin crash site

3   North Weald Bassett
     Airfield

4   Oakmere Park, Potters Bar
     L31 Zeppelin crash site

5   Monkhams Hall, Waltham Abbey
     AA gun emplacement

6   Chingford
     Airfield

7   One Tree Hill, Southwark
     AA gun emplacement

Map of southern England showing the sites investigated by the Great War Archaeology Group during the First Blitz Project (2005–07). (Dave Hibbitt for GWAG)

knowledge of, and extensive contacts in, north-west Norfolk. Between them, they were hoping to unravel the mystery of Hunstanton's role in the anti-Zeppelin war. The fragments of information they had gleaned did not fit together; there seemed to be too many different installations reputed to have been involved. 'There seems to be a profusion of buildings,' Jim had emailed Chris, listing up to six cited in documentary sources as possible locations for wireless direction-finding equipment in and around Hunstanton during the war. The problem was that wartime secrecy had sown post-war confusion. Too few people were involved at the time, and too little was reliably recorded, for post-war researchers to be able to work out what had actually been going on. Even long after the war, the authorities were sensitive. The prolific author and journalist Harold Begbie was warned off publishing his *Wireless in the War, 1914–1918* – it still exists only as an unpublished manuscript.

An aerial view along the cliffs at Hunstanton. Though the cliffs rise only about 20m above the sea, they are high by Norfolk standards, and the site looks out over The Wash and the North Sea beyond. This was a perfect spot for a wireless listening station to track the movements of German warships, submarines, and airships. (Courtesy of Mike Page)

An aerial view of the cliffs at Old Hunstanton in Norfolk, showing the whitewashed Victorian lighthouse of 1840, the redbrick coastguard tower, the coastguard cottages behind, and the distinctive cliffs themselves formed of layers of red chalk, white chalk, and brown carrstone. This, ninety years ago, was the frontline in a new global technological war. (Courtesy of Mike Page)

The intelligence war was so secret because Britain and Germany were locked into a technological arms-race. Wireless communication was as new as flight. The popular image of the First World War is of the mud, barbed wire, machine-guns and heavy artillery of the trenches. Historians have focused on the great battles of attrition on the Western Front. They have paid very little attention to the electronic technological revolution that was transforming the nature of war.

The twenty-one-year-old Guglielmo Marconi had arrived in Britain in February 1896, and by August of that year the War Office had arranged a conference to discuss the military implications of his invention of wireless. Marconi demonstrated his equipment by transmitting a signal over a distance of 20 yards between two adjoining rooms. Further experiments and demonstrations followed, and in 1899 five sets of wireless equipment were sent for service in the Boer War. Though mishandled in South Africa, the Admiralty was convinced of the new technology's potential, placing an order for a further twenty-six sets for use on Royal Navy ships and six for stations on the British coast.

In the years before the First World War, the military tried many experiments in wireless communication with equipment installations on land, at sea, and in the air. It was the air that presented the greatest technical challenge. The main problem was the wireless spark transmitter, which presented a potential fire hazard, as the aircraft were constructed from highly flammable materials. Then there was the weight and bulk: a hefty 200lbs of equipment was needed to generate sufficient power to operate the wireless when airborne – a major disadvantage in the lightweight, low-powered aeroplanes of the day. Most, also, were single-seaters, so the pilot was expected to fly the aeroplane, make and record aerial reconnaissances, and tap out messages with a Morse key strapped to his knee. It is easy to understand the British General Grierson's comment after training manoeuvres in August 1912: 'The airship was of more use to me than the aeroplane, as being fitted with wireless telegraphy, I received messages in a continuous stream, and immediately after the observation was made.'

But it was the Germans – not the British – who were developing the airship into a major weapon of war. And, though it was the British military and postal services that had supported Marconi's experiments, German engineers had been able to keep abreast because much technical information was published in specialist periodicals in the years before the war. The German company Telefunken had emerged as a major world rival of Marconi, competing directly for maritime contracts for wireless communication. In fact, in January 1911, to overcome licensing and other contract difficulties, Telefunken, Marconi and a Belgian company had formed a new syndicate, in which the majority share was held by the former.

So Britain and Germany shared knowledge of the evolving technology, and as late as July 1914 Marconi and Telefunken engineers exchanged visits. The two great powers were on a par in wireless communications. It was as well for the Germans that this was so. One of the first British acts of war was to cut the German links to the transatlantic telephone cables. This forced Germany to rely on wireless technology as her only means of communicating with her far-flung colonies, with America, and, most importantly, with her shipping. The British move seems to have been anticipated, however, since the power of the wireless transmitter at Nauen, just outside Berlin, had been considerably increased by the outbreak of war.

Wartime use of the airwaves to transmit information opened other chapters in technological warfare, with attempts to block enemy communications by transmitting on the same frequency (jamming), to intercept and read enemy communications (leading to signal encryption and code-breaking), and to feed false information into the enemy communication network.

But in the short run the British authorities were caught unprepared for the hurried change in German communication strategy: it was not until late in 1914 that Captain William Hall and Sir Alfred Ewing established what was to become the famous Room 40 in the Admiralty Old Building. By the time the Zeppelin War reached its climax in the late summer of 1916, Room 40 had become the humming nerve-centre of home defence. Telegraph messages would pass from wireless direction-finding stations on the coast to the telegraph office in the Admiralty basement. From here, the messages, written out but still in code, would be sent up the pneumatic tube that connected the basement telegraphy office with Room 40 above, where they dropped into a waiting basket. Here, in this top-secret room and its adjoining offices, worked a department of code-breakers.

When a major raid was imminent, as the Zeppelin fleet massed and moved out across the North Sea, messages would pour in from stations along the east coast as they intercepted wireless transmissions from the airships. Room 40's decrypts – coupled with simple triangulation of readings from separate stations – enabled the Admiralty to track enemy movements and alert the British defenders. 'Take air raid action': the instruction would pass down telephone lines to observer posts, searchlight emplacements, gun sites, and fighter airfields. Wireless direction-finding was the radar of the First Blitz. The most important station was the one Jim Lewis and Chris Mackie were looking for: that at Hunstanton on The Wash.

Zeppelins had the advantage of being able to fly high, and the later height-climbers were able to rise over 20,000ft to keep clear of attacking aircraft and guns. But at these heights, with equipment failing, crews debilitated, and independent navigation impossible, the airships became useless. When the crippled L48 lost her way on the night of 17 June 1917, she contacted a home wireless station for bearings. A Zeppelin wishing to find its position would usually call the German control centre at Cuxhaven, giving its particular call sign, normally a single letter, and request permission to obtain a bearing. The message would be encrypted and delivered in Morse code. Once permission was granted, the Zeppelin would transmit the letter 'V', which the wireless operator would repeat for about thirty seconds. The Zeppelin's signal would be picked up by at least three fixed German wireless direction-finding stations, and the respective bearing between each of these and the airship would be taken.

But others were also listening – at a string of British direction-finding stations along the east coast. What Jim and Chris's research had uncovered was something of the top-secret intelligence war that was being fought on the north-west Norfolk coast ninety years ago. In local archives Chris had come across a copy of a 1907 edition of *Electrical Engineering* in which readers were informed that the Post Office had built two new wireless stations on The Wash, one at Skegness on the east side, the other at Hunstanton on the west. The 15½ miles of wireless service between them was designed to replace 90 miles of telegraphic land-line. The installations, which were identical, comprised a 122ft-high mast built of planks bolted together in a design 'very pliable in high winds, yet exceedingly strong'. The mast was stepped in concrete and stabilised by three sets of four stays tied to ground anchors formed of long bolts set in deeply buried oak beams. The receiver at the top of the mast was connected by a set of six air-wires to the telegraphic apparatus room lodged in the coastguard tower. The engine and alternator were installed in a wooden outhouse. 'Both stations,'

Bayntun Hippisley, a wireless enthusiast who, with colleague Edward Clarke, reported to the Admiralty in 1914 that they were receiving German naval messages on a lower wavelength than any being picked up by the existing Marconi stations. Hippisley was commissioned to upgrade the Hunstanton station.

Electrical Engineer explained, 'pick up messages from a variety of sources, and both are able to receive, on occasion, from the great Telefunken station of Nauen, near Berlin…'

The Admiralty had been involved from the beginning, allowing the coastguard station to be used, and providing naval personnel to man the post, working in six-hour shifts of three men. But by the time war broke out, the technology had moved on. Bayntun Hippisley and Edward Clarke, two wireless enthusiasts, reported to the Admiralty that they were receiving German naval messages on a lower wavelength than any being picked up by the existing Marconi stations. Hippisley was a landowner, a former army officer, and, unusually for a man of his class, a trained mechanical and electrical engineer. In 1913 he had served on the War Office Committee on Wireless Telegraphy, and at the outbreak of war he had joined Naval Intelligence and been made a commander. He clearly knew what he was talking about. Sir Alfred Ewing, busy with William Hall building his cryptographic department in Room 40, authorised Hippisley and Clarke to set up a new listening station at Hunstanton. The station became known as 'Hippisley's Hut'.

The 'Hippisley Hut' in Old Hunstanton. Was this the site of a new listening station? Or, more likely, was it part of a cliff-top installation that was moved here after the First World War? The two single-storey extensions on either side of this holiday let may be two huts (or one cut in two?) that once played a role in Britain's secret war against the German Zeppelins. (Chris Mackie)

But where was it? Delving into the archives, Jim and Chris had discovered records of several places in and around Old Hunstanton where Hippisley had supposedly established 'secret wireless listening devices'. Chris, on the other hand, knew of a local landmark dubbed the 'Hippisley Hut', which lay in a quiet street of the old town a short distance from the cliffs. The site is a curio: a cobbled drive leads to a large, two-storey, weather-boarded holiday chalet, with a veranda along the front and single-storey wooden huts adjoining at either end. One (or both) of the huts is assumed to be the original 'Hippisley Hut' (or 'Huts'). But why here? The location makes no sense. Whatever Hippisley's innovations, he surely made use of the 122ft-tall receiver already in place on the cliffs, and, presumably, the engine and alternator.

Strangely, perhaps, in view of the secrecy in which the Intelligence war was later shrouded, contemporary photographs have survived – some reproduced in *Electrical Engineering*, others on picture postcards – that depict the coastal station before 1914. These show, in addition to

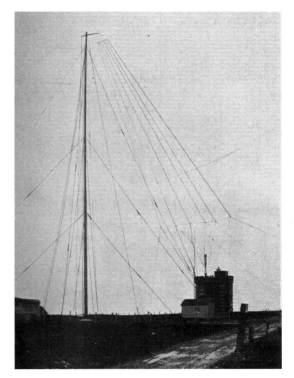

Electrical Engineering magazine featured this image of the Hunstanton coastguard station and the associated wireless receiver mast and connecting wires on 14 February 1907. Information about wireless technology was soon to become top secret, but the magazine published a series of images about the technology in a three-page article entitled 'Wireless Technology Across The Wash'.

the surviving lighthouse, coastguard tower, and coastguard cottages, at least three single-storey buildings on the cliffs, probably timber-built, all now vanished. It seems likely that this was always the place, and either Hippisley built a new installation here, or one of the existing buildings came subsequently to be known as the 'Hippisley Hut' through association with him. This one at least was recycled after the war. Single-storey timber buildings are relatively easy to dismantle, transport and re-erect on a new site. Part at least of what was once a top-secret First World War Intelligence-gathering station seems to have been moved a mile or so inland and become a holiday let.

But we are left guessing. We need to survey and to dig. Below ground, almost certainly, there are answers to some of the questions about Britain's high-tech war against the Zeppelins. The land is owned by King's Lynn and West Norfolk Borough Council. The area depends heavily on tourism and is keen to promote its heritage. But when the Great War Archaeology Group approached the council for permission

Here, *Electrical Engineering* reveals the interior of the apparatus room at Hunstanton. This appears to be within a wooden structure – rather than the coastguard tower itself. (The German military had no need to subscribe to the magazine. The British-based Marconi company and the German-based Telefunken were exchanging visits and sharing technical information as late as the summer of 1914.)

to investigate the site, they met a wall of indifference and obstruction. The group was expected to obtain clearance from no fewer than a dozen separate council departments and other authorities – some of whom remained resolutely un-contactable when approached – in order to qualify for a licence to carry out any work. Life is short, and time is precious – especially for a volunteer group without paid staff. Knowing this, and keen to support heritage research in the local community, councils elsewhere have provided a single line of communication in dealing with permissions to carry out fieldwork. King's Lynn and West Norfolk Borough Council, by contrast, has effectively blocked archaeological investigation of the Hunstanton cliffs site by placing it bureaucratically beyond reach. One day, because of coastal erosion, it will fall into the sea. Will it by then have been investigated?

Jim Lewis had hoped to bring the rest of the team up to explore the site. A geophysical survey might have located the footings of buildings, masts, and anchors. Targeted excavation might then have added essential details about form and date. The layout of Hippisley's wireless direction-finding station might have been recovered. Still, he knew a lot more

In this 1907 view, we see some of the new-fangled wiring connecting the wireless receiver mast with the coastguard tower.

Another view inside an apparatus room, this time that at Skegness, on the opposite side of The Wash. Soon such information would be entirely embargoed. Indeed, such were the walls of secrecy built around wireless technology once war broke out that the historical record of what went on remains incomplete and contradictory to this day. Archaeology is helping to reveal the secrets of this little-known technological war.

from his desktop research than when he started. It was clear that all the time, throughout the war, the British coastal stations were listening for noise on the air-waves and sending messages received from German warships, submarines and airships down the wire to the Admiralty in London. There, messages were decoded, positions triangulated, movements tracked, speeds calculated, and targets predicted.

By summer 1916, the system had been perfected. When 'the Zepps' came over, the home defences had been alerted by central command. Air crew had been scrambled and the fighters were on their patrol lines in the air above. Ground observers were listening for the characteristic drone of airship engines, watching for the distinctive cigar-silhouettes in the upper sky. Searchlights and AA guns were manned and ready, waiting for targets, waiting for the chance to engage 'the baby-killers'. The secret Intelligence war of wireless operators and code-breakers made it all possible. They were an essential part of a new, high-tech, twentieth-century battle for air supremacy in the skies over Britain. It is a story we are only just beginning to tell.

5

London's Ring of Iron

Desktop research: it is the very backbone of archaeological excavation. From our desks we aim to find out as much as possible about a site before taking a team into the field to investigate it. There is no point in going to all the time and trouble of doing fieldwork to find out things already known. There is no point digging a site that was completely excavated twenty-five years ago. Nor one shown to have been trashed by modern ploughing.

We generally start by checking the county Historic Environment Record (HER). This offers a comprehensive list of what is known from antiquarian research, chance finds, fieldwalking surveys, crop-marks seen on air photographs, and any earlier excavations that may have taken place. We have another look at the air photographs to see if there is anything not noticed before. We track down old maps to check whether lost buildings, earthworks and field boundaries are shown. We find out what other people have written about the place, and we follow up leads to important documents held at the county record office or an archive elsewhere. If field archaeology is a scientific experiment, the aim of good desktop research is to avoid repeating an experiment the results of which are known, and to ensure that new experiments are as effectively targeted and structured as possible.

The closer we come to the present, the larger 'desktop' looms in our research programmes. The reason is simple: the archives are much fuller for the recent past. The archaeology of modern conflict has to be deeply embedded in historical research. The First World War is recorded in millions of surviving documents, maps and photographs. Yet the record is incomplete, and archaeology has the potential to fill many gaps; but first we need to know where the gaps are. When Great War Archaeology Group members contacted The National Archives at Kew in south-west London to find out if there were any records of 1914–18 air-war defences, they obtained an old Ordnance Survey map, hand-dated to 1917, showing Greater London and the surrounding countryside.

Although rather faded and a bit rubbed around the edges, this map was to prove invaluable. The immediately striking thing was that it had been marked with a profusion of hand-drawn green and yellow dots. Each dot varied in diameter from around 3–6mm, thus covering areas of several miles on the map's surface. There was no legend to explain what the coloured dots represented. Instead of being a comprehensive record of air defences in and around London at a specific moment in time, the map – drawn up for some particular, and now unknown, purpose – merely offered some cryptic clues.

Jim Lewis, GWAG's industrial historian, and Dave Hibbitt, one of the group's two geophysical surveyors, already knew enough, however, to guess what the dots meant: the yellow ones were searchlights, the green were anti-aircraft guns. Jim and Dave were reasonably confident of this because desktop research was already well advanced when the map turned up, and Jim's local knowledge helped recognise that several of the green dots were in roughly the same place as known anti-aircraft gun emplacements of the period.

GWAG had decided to focus its investigation on the Lea Valley area of north-east London. Unless exploring a particular site to glean specific data, archaeology tends to involve sampling. Archaeologists do not dig up every Roman villa, for example, and of those that are investigated it is rare to excavate the whole thing. Even broader landscape studies are delimited to specific study areas. The First Blitz Project was the first systematic investigation of the 1914–18 air war through its material remains. We were involved in pioneering work in uncharted territory. The danger was that we would end up collecting random bits of information from here and there, and that no meaningful patterns would emerge. It was essential to define a study area – a geographical sample – and to seek to plot all the sites within that area. This would create a detailed picture of the intensity and character of the home-defence network. Hence our decision to investigate an area extending 40km north from the Thames, and approximately 40km east–west, centred on the Lea Valley. The plan was to carry out a thorough desktop survey to plot all the sites within this area, and then to home in on selected sites for detailed investigation on the ground.

Jim Lewis was in his element. This was home turf. He has some claim to being the leading expert on the industrial history of the Lea Valley. He and Dave Hibbitt set about plotting the locations of all known First World War airfields, gun emplacements, searchlight batteries, armaments factories, munitions works, and explosives plants. They started with the war industries, which, along with key service installations like gasworks, waterworks and electric power plants, were the potential targets of air raids. Just south of what is now the North Circular Road in Edmonton was the British Oxygen Company works, which had manufactured the incendiary bullets used by Royal Flying Corps pilots to attack Zeppelins. The bullets were given the rather charming name of 'Sparklet', after the popular soda siphon bulb manufactured by the company. A few hundred metres north was the Eley Cartridge Works, where a range of mainly small-arms ammunition was manufactured. Further north, about a mile up the valley, was the Ponders End Shell Works, again critical to the war effort. Around a mile north again was the Royal Small Arms Factory at Enfield Lock; now a housing estate, it had been founded in 1816, was the birthplace of the famous Lee Enfield rifle, the standard British issue of the First World War, and was also the manufacturer of many other small arms, including the Lewis gun, the principal British light machine-gun of the war.

A mile north of the Royal Small Arms Factory was the Essex town of Waltham Abbey. This was home to the Royal Gunpowder Mills, established in the eighteenth century. At its height during the First World War, the 'powder-mills' employed over 6,000 munitions workers. The factory is now a tourist attraction. During the war it was a premier site for the manufacture of the explosive cordite, used by the ton in the production of shells for the Western Front. Just east of Waltham Abbey town centre was the Nobel Works – another factory responsible for mass-producing incendiary and other ammunition that was used particularly by the Royal Flying Corps. There were even hints of a chemical warfare plant: it was rumoured that experiments with, or production of, poison gas had taken place at Ponders End in Enfield.

In 1914–18 the Lea Valley was at the heart of the British war economy. What would happen if a Zeppelin dropped a cargo of bombs on one of its plants? The defence of the Lea Valley was clearly a priority. It also lay beneath the principal approach line of enemy bombers heading for the centre of the capital. The Zeppelins usually came directly across the North Sea from their North German bases, making landfall over East Anglia, then veered south-west to attack London, with the West End, the City, and the East End docks prime targets. Everything pointed, therefore, to a heavy concentration of lights, guns and fighter aircraft in and around the Lea Valley.

But not at first. The war started with British mishap. The developed system was probably in place by the summer of 1916, but before then the state of London's air defences had caused much anguish. Charles Ffoulkes, Curator of the Tower of London Armouries, described the 'Dad's Army' muddle of 1914 in his autobiography:

> Kitchener's Army and Territorials came to draw what arms were left in the Tower and often had to be content with old patterns or even in some cases with gas barrels on wood stocks used only for drill purposes. This state of urgency seemed to suggest that middle-aged men might be useful to replace the home men needed overseas. There was much talk, literally 'in the air', about possible attack by Zeppelin airships, and as a defence a small gun was mounted on the Foreign Office manned by the Artillery. For some unexplained reason, possibly the urgent need for gunners in France, the project was abandoned, and in alarm the Lord Mayor, according to current reports, appealed to Mr. Churchill, then First Lord of the Admiralty. As one might have expected, Churchill acted and acted rapidly.

He did indeed. At this time the defence of London was a Navy responsibility (only in February 1916 did it devolve to the Army), though Churchill's options were limited: twenty-eight of the thirty-three AA guns available to him at the beginning of the war were completely useless 1pdr 'pom-poms'. Everything needed for London's defence – men, guns, equipment, transport, munitions, supplies – was in short supply in the early months. Rather, the Western Front was the first priority when war broke out, and indeed for its duration. GWAG's desktop research revealed that the wartime air-defence system was the result of two years of improvisation, trial and error, and slow build-up. It was something of the finished system that the map from the National Archives had depicted.

Jim Lewis and Dave Hibbitt decided to turn the data they had collected into a single big map, showing the Lea Valley area's factories and defences (see colour plate 5). The information was plotted onto a modern map at 1:50,000 scale, with Waltham Abbey positioned towards the centre as a starting point. A computer-generated 'virtual layer' was then placed accurately over the top and tied to known points like roads and towns. Thereafter, all the information gathered from documentary sources was transferred onto the map, a task that took several long days, even using a range of professional software programmes for image editing and setting.

The plotting of the sites on the map revealed patterns – most crucially the shape of the first system of defence against strategic bombing in the history of warfare. The war factories lay alongside or close to the river Lea, probably because the river, linked with the Thames and the East End docks, was used for transporting raw materials and manufactured goods. The river would also once have been used for power. One of the main reasons for the location of the Royal Small Arms Factory at Enfield Lock was that here there was sufficient head and flow of water to drive the water-wheels that used to power machinery in the barrel mill.

A series of gun emplacements had been erected on the high ground on the eastern side of the Lea Valley – at Folly Lane, Walthamstow, Pole Hill, Chingford, and Monkhams Hall and Colemans Lane, Waltham Abbey. These guns belonged to one of seven 'Control Areas' of London District Anti-Aircraft (AA) Command, and were manned by 14 AA Company RGA (Royal Garrison Artillery). They formed part of a thick inner belt of guns deployed in the suburban areas around Central London. A second, outer ring of guns was deployed in a wide circle in the countryside beyond the city limits. The guns were 3in (or 6pdr) quick-firers (QF), mounted to be able to traverse through 360° and to elevate up to a vertical position. Firing fifteen rounds a minute to a maximum vertical range of 18,000ft, the dense network of guns guarding London had the capacity to fill the sky with bursting shrapnel.

But the guns needed to see their targets. Searchlights became the gunners' night sight. Most of the searchlights seem to have been deployed in a ring between the inner and outer gun lines, but there was also a small concentration in Central London itself, where they were often placed on the tops of tall buildings. There appeared to be no guns located near to searchlights, which would make sense, as the searchlights would stand out as highly visible targets, inviting aerial attack when illuminated.

The searchlight had been around for about thirty-five years, its development having been sponsored by the Navy and trialled at Chatham in 1879 by the company Siemens, Wilde and Sautter. By the First World War, Siemens had developed a new generation of more powerful carbon-arc lights, and it was probably these that were deployed. Because the Zeppelins attacked at night, searchlights quickly became an essential feature of the first strategic bombing campaign. Once an air-raid warning was given and the approach of enemy airships anticipated, the searchlights snapped on and sent up shafts of light that arced across the sky, the shafts converging into a cone once a raider had been spotted, trapping the airship in a moving point of deadly illumination.

Jim and Dave found evidence for thirty-three AA guns and nineteen searchlights in GWAG's 40km by 40km Lea Valley study area. But all the evidence implies that the guns claimed few victims. To pinpoint a target 10 or 15,000ft away in three-dimensional space, one moving through a night sky, was less than straightforward. The danger, in any case, was too obvious: on clear nights airship captains would avoid passing over London at low altitudes, preferring to hover on the fringes awaiting their opportunity. But this, for that very reason, was the killing-zone of the British night-fighters.

The airfields were also plotted on the big map. Barely a decade after the Wright brothers first achieved sustained and controlled powered flight at Kitty Hawk in the USA in December 1903, fields around London where cattle and sheep had grazed were converted into the airfields of the new techno-war in the sky, with grass runways, wooden hangers, and brick-built offices, workshops and barracks. The Royal Naval Air Service had an airfield at Chingford (now the site of Thames Water's William Girling reservoir), and No.39 Home Defence Squadron of the Army's Royal Flying Corps was distributed across three West Essex airfields, Hainault Farm, Suttons Farm (Hornchurch), and North Weald Bassett. The pilots of 39 Squadron, a unit of dedicated home-defence fighters, emerged in the late summer of 1916 as an elite of Zepp-killers: Lieutenant William Leefe Robinson shot down SL11 on 3 September; Lieutenant Frederick Sowrey shot down L32 on 24 September; and Lieutenant Wulfstan Tempest shot down L31 on 2 October.

That summer of 1916 the skies above the Lea Valley, which had long been the preferred approach corridor of Zeppelin raiders heading for London, were transformed into a zone of lethal danger and decisive combat. Jim and Dave plotted the crash sites of SL11 at Cuffley and L31 at Potters Bar on their big map. Had they extended eastwards, they might have shown L32 at South Green and L33 at Little Wigborough (the latter the only kill of the anti-aircraft guns, one of whose shells exploded inside the hull, inflicting mortal damage, though without setting the airship ablaze). The group's chosen study area turned out to represent the very heart of the battle. The question now was: how much would survive on the ground?

6
Lights and Guns

In June 2006 Dave Hibbitt and Angie Cannon were on the hill at Monkhams Hall just north of Waltham Abbey where, ninety years before, gunners had manned one of the 3in quick-firer anti-aircraft guns guarding the north-western approaches to London. A prominent, rounded eminence, the hill rises steeply about the Lea Valley. The valley itself – a belt of light industry and modern suburbs – stretches away southwards, penetrating deeply into east London. On the horizon Dave and Angie could see familiar landmarks representing Canary Wharf, the City, the South Bank, and the West End. As they looked down the line of the Lea into the heart of London, they were observing what had once been the principal Zeppelin approach corridor.

Just east of the river were other spurs of high ground similar to the hill at Monkhams. These include Pole Hill, about 4½ miles away, where they knew another anti-aircraft gun had been sited. It was easy, on such a viewpoint, for the imagination to take flight: there would have been the distant drone of the airship engines, the sinister cigar-silhouette drifting south, shafts of light soaring and searching from a dozen pinpricks on the ground, the rapid-fire booming of the guns, and the starbursts of exploding shrapnel in the sky.

Today, Monkhams Hall, with its stable block and other associated buildings, lies a few hundred metres north-west of the gun emplacement, which still stands, now ruined, on the top of the hill. The hall is probably mainly of mid-late nineteenth-century date, and its buildings have now been converted into a series of separate residences. Yet it seems likely that the hall would have had a military use during the First World War. Was

Monkhams Hall anti-aircraft gun emplacement ('Structure A'). This view from the north-east shows the position of the gun on a prominent hilltop overlooking the Lea Valley (with modern factories clearly visible in the background). As well as forming part of a line of guns protecting the war industries of the Lea Valley, Monkhams was also part of a broad ring of guns that covered the approaches to London. (Nadia Durrani for GWAG)

the HQ office and telephone link here? Were there billets for the gunners – perhaps two dozen men in all – stationed on the hill?

The site of the gun emplacement itself was certainly part of the Monkhams Hall estate, and possibly lay within a walled garden: fragments of a substantial brick boundary wall survive to the north, and there are various mounds of overgrown earth and rubble which perhaps represent the remains of non-military structures. Most of the hill now belongs to the Corporation of London, and is maintained as 'buffer land' designed to limit development in the vicinity of Epping Forest. It is therefore managed by forest keepers, and general public access is permitted. Through the good offices of Keith French, Head Forest Keeper for the North of Epping Forest, GWAG had been granted permission to investigate the site, and the grass had been cut over an extensive area around the gun emplacement and the various earth-and-rubble mounds nearby.

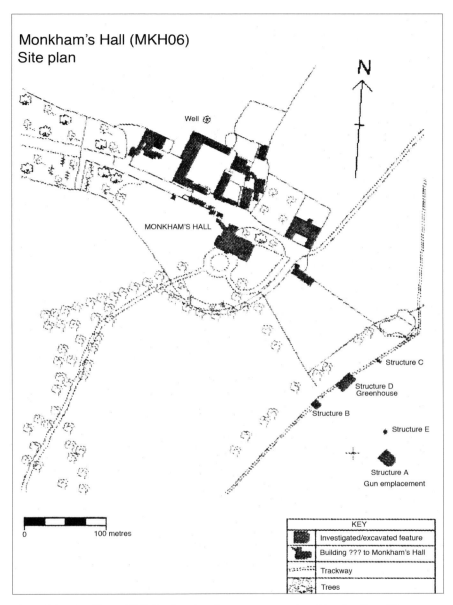

Plan of the Monkhams Hall site showing the structures explored by the Great War Archaeology Group in relation to contemporary buildings and other landscape features shown on maps of the period. (Fizz Altinoluk for GWAG)

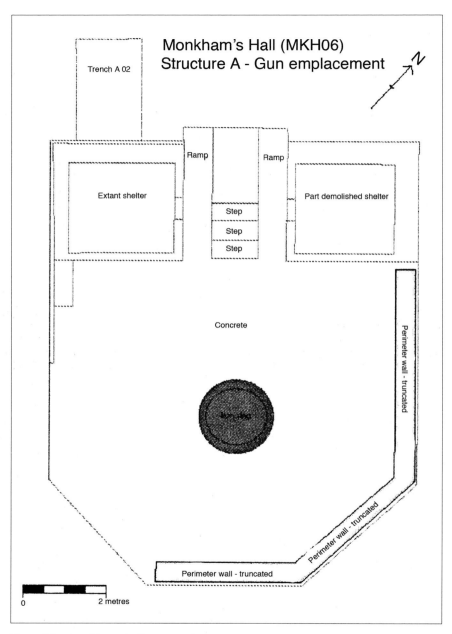

Plan of the Monkhams Hall gun emplacement – Structure A. (Fizz Altinoluk for GWAG)

1 A selection of grommets, rivets, and fragments of airframe (all aluminium alloy) from Zeppelin L48, metal-detected from plough-soil on the crash-site in Crofts Field, Theberton Hall Farm, Suffolk. The rivets are sheared in half, the airframe fragments have been twisted and torn apart, and several of the grommets still have carbonised fabric trapped within their back folds – demonstrating the force with which L48 hit the ground. (Julian Evan-Hart for GWAG)

2 One of the first items detected from the field at Theberton was this officer's button made of copper alloy (with possible traces of silvering). Note the twisted rope and anchor emblem of the German Imperial Navy. It shows signs of intense burning. Dimension: 19mm diameter. (Julian Evan-Hart for GWAG)

3 An archive postcard of *c.*1910 showing the lighthouse at Old Hunstanton in Norfolk, with the coastguard tower clearly in view, and the masts and connecting wires of the Marconi wireless direction–finding station, which was at the cutting edge of the secret war to track the movements of German warships, submarines and airships. (Courtesy of Chris Mackie)

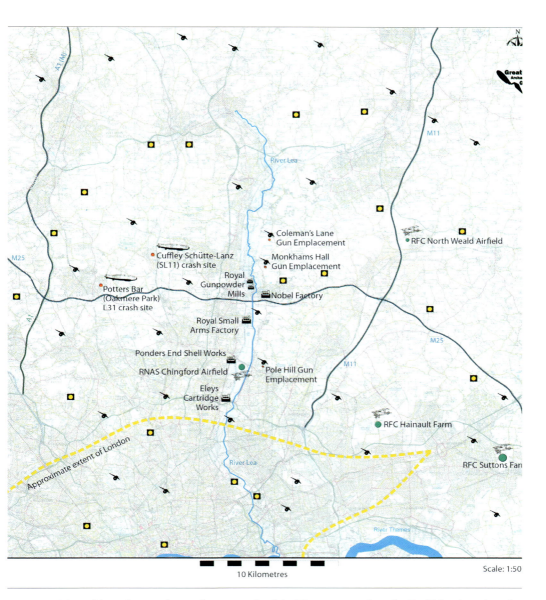

Map labels:

A1 (M)

M11

River Lea

M11

M25

A1

M25

Coleman's Lane
Gun Emplacement

RFC North Weald Airfield

Cuffley Schütte-Lanz
(SL11) crash site

Monkhams Hall
Gun Emplacement

Royal
Gunpowder
Mills

Potters Bar
(Oakmere Park)
L31 crash site

Nobel Factory

Royal Small
Arms Factory

Ponders End Shell Works

RNAS Chingford Airfield

Pole Hill Gun
Emplacement

Eleys
Cartridge
Works

RFC Hainault Farm

Approximate extent of London

River Lea

RFC Suttons Farm

River Thames

10 Kilometres

Scale: 1:50

5 Map of the 40km x 40km study area north of the Thames centred on the Lea Valley investigated by the Great War Archaeology Group during the First Blitz Project. The most striking thing about the landscape to be revealed is the intensity of the militarisation that had taken place by the summer of 1916 – a testimony, perhaps, to the effectiveness of the German bombers as terror weapons. (Dave Hibbitt and Jim Lewis for GWAG; base map ©Crown Copyright. Reproduced by permission of Ordnance Survey®)

Opposite below: 4 A modern shot of the Old Hunstanton lighthouse and coastguard tower, taken from approximately the same position as the archive postcard view. So little is known about the wireless direction-finding station on the site, it is regrettable that the local council has refused co-operation with efforts to investigate the site archaeologically. (Courtesy of Chris Mackie)

6 The steel gun-ring on the anti-aircraft gun emplacement at Monkhams Hall in Essex, after clearance and cleaning. This particular ring, however, dates from the Second World War. (Nadia Durrani for GWAG)

7 A false alarm! It looked a bit like an unexploded shell, so the police were called to guard the site pending the arrival of the bomb-disposal squad at Monkhams Hall. It turned out to be a table leg. The expert opinion was that it was better to be safe than sorry, and for the archaeologists it was a reminder that ammunition from the First World War, especially on the Western Front, continues to kill every year. A feature of modern industrialised warfare is that the abundant material remains it leaves behind are sometimes still lethal. (Nadia Durrani for GWAG)

8 The Theberton excavation of the crash-site of Zeppelin L48 in June 2006. After the topsoil was machine-stripped, archaeologists and metal-detectorists began cleaning back and searching for evidence of an entry hole of heavy metal components. (Nadia Durrani for GWAG)

9 Metal-detectorist Jeff Evans examines a find on the Zeppelin crash-site at Theberton. (Nadia Durrani for GWAG)

10 The archaeological finds-tray after the first day of excavation at Theberton, containing an assortment of fragments of Zeppelin L48 – aluminium sheeting, bits of girder, fabric grommets, rivets, eyelets, and much else. (Nadia Durrani for GWAG)

11 In the dappled light at the end of a summer's day, sitting in an English barley field, project director Neil Faulkner speaks to camera of the death and destruction that the Theberton site represents. (Nadia Durrani for GWAG)

12 A poignant setting: poppies sway in the foreground while the excavation gets underway in the background. The archaeology of the First World War generates a succession of experiences and images rich in symbolism. (Nadia Durrani for GWAG)

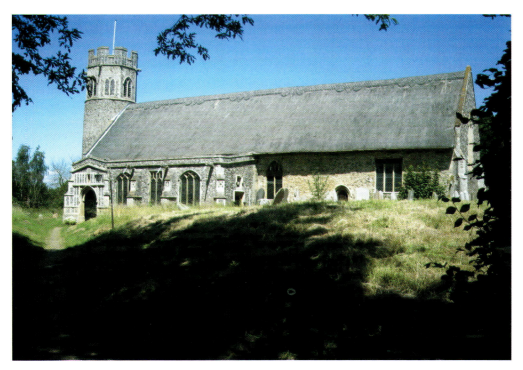

13 The pretty parish church at Theberton – with an exceptionally rare thatched roof. It contains a large piece of the crashed Zeppelin in its porch. Its cemetery contains a memorial to the German airmen who died on L48. This picture-postcard image of rural England is a reminder that the First Blitz transformed the nature of war by turning the entire homeland – its industries, settlements, and people – into a military target. (Nadia Durrani for GWAG)

14 Zeppelin L48 under attack by British fighter aircraft in the skies over Suffolk in the early hours of 17 June 1917. Note the half-light of approaching dawn – fatal to the Zeppelin, which was essentially a stealth-bomber, dependent for protection on the cover of dark nights. Note, too, the huge size of the airship, contrasting with that of its attackers, the two fighter planes shown left and right. (An original image by Ray Rimell for the cover of *The Last Flight of the L48*, used with permission of the copyright holders, Albatross Publications Ltd)

The gun emplacement viewed from the north. Other spurs of high ground along the eastern edge of the Lea Valley – where further guns were positioned – can be seen in the background. The view is of the back of the emplacement, with one shelter standing, the other (in the foreground) largely demolished and overgrown with nettles and weeds. (Nadia Durrani for GWAG)

The grass-cutting was paid for by the BBC. This was lucky, since our GWAG field team is made up of volunteers and we generally operate on a shoestring. GWAG includes both 'academic' and 'professional' archaeologists (this being the curious terminology used to distinguish between university-based archaeologists and those working for commercial rescue-units). We contribute our skills, time, and, to a degree, resources. Dave and Angie are professional geophysical surveyors and have all their own equipment, but on a GWAG project, everything they do, including bringing in a lot of high-tech equipment, is a voluntary contribution to research. Anything extra – including cutting grass, using heavy machinery, pumping out water – means special funding. Fortunately, television – for the time being anyway – has an appetite for modern conflict archaeology. BBC2's *Timewatch* was making a documentary on the First Blitz, and they gave GWAG a small grant to facilitate the archaeology. Among other things it got the grass cut at Monkhams. The geofizz team

Structure A looking from the north-west up the ramp and steps onto the gun platform. (Nadia Durrani for GWAG)

were then able to get in and survey the site. The tight filming schedule did not allow for the pre-excavation survey that would usually be carried out several days in advance of excavation. Consequently, it would have to be done alongside the metal-detecting and excavations; a situation with which Dave and Angie were to become very familiar.

To geofizz they used electrical resistance surveying equipment, which involves feeding an electrical current into the ground and measuring resistance to the current's flow. Buried wall foundations, concrete floors, and spreads of rubble, for example, offer high resistance to the current. Silted-up ditches and soil-filled pits, on the other hand, because they are generally wetter, offer low resistance. The trick is to record the differences systematically over a large area and to plot the successive readings, so that buried features become visible in the patterning of low and high resistance areas. To achieve this, a grid of tapes must be laid out, tied into known visible features in the landscape, ideally features shown on OS maps, and readings must then be taken at regular intervals.

The resistance meter equipment – in this case a TR Systems model – has a bar with two metal probes projecting from the bottom. These probes are pushed into the ground to generate an electric current below the surface,

On Structure A we excavated one corner of the fill of the demolished shelter, seeking to confirm that it was identical with the one still standing, and that nothing of significance had been buried in situ. The fill comprised a uniform deposit of rubble – containing shrews' nests, which caused work to cease. (Nadia Durrani for GWAG)

and a resistance reading is then taken automatically by the equipment's internal data-logger. Resistivity surveys can be slow and tedious because of the need to repeatedly drive the probes into the ground, extract them, and move them forwards each time a new reading is taken. It did not help that the Monkhams site is formed of London clay, notorious among field archaeologists for the way in which it more or less bakes into concrete in the sun, or turns into heavy claggy mud in the wet. To survey just over half a hectare of ground at an intensity of one reading per metre – usually two hours' work – took Dave and Angie two full days. By the end of it they had taken 5,837 readings – one for every square metre of ground covered. The data were downloaded and previewed on site on a laptop computer running TR Systems software. The idea now was to tweak the imaging to bring up contrasts, smooth out rough edges, and generally create a picture that actually looked like something to ordinary field archaeologists, rather than just to the trained eyes of a geophysicist. At this point they could be saved as TIFF files and copies run off to assist in making informed decisions on site.

All this took time. While it was happening, the rest of the field team got started on the gun emplacement. We first cleared it of litter, vegetation, and loose debris. It comprises a raised platform of brick and concrete with a large inset steel ring (1.8m in diameter) in the middle as a gun mounting. The basic shape is a square 8m x 8m across with a polygonal projection on the forward (south-eastern) face. On the opposite (north-western) side of the platform are two brick shelters, the northern one largely demolished and rubble-filled, the western one substantially intact (though demolition had begun about a year before the dig and been stopped only by the protest of a local resident). The shelters, which appear to have been identical, were 1.75m high, and were built of brick walls with reinforced concrete roofs. Between the two shelters was a set of steps with twin ramps either side leading up onto the platform. Close to the north-west side of the structure, amid rubble debris, lying on or projecting from the surface, were a small iron wheel, fragments of barbed wire, and a 'corkscrew' barbed-wire support. Presumably the gun emplacement had once been surrounded by a barbed-wire fence.

As well as general clearance, we excavated out part of the fill in the ruined northern shelter – before work was suspended after the discovery of shrews' nests in the rubble – and also a small 2.5m x 1.5m trench extending from the north-western side of the platform. The whole structure was then planned and photographed. Several things had become apparent, and further research since has refined the observations made at the time. First, at least three main phases of work seem to be represented. The platform and shelters are built of old dull-red bricks, and the basic structure is known to date from the First World War. But there is later work – such as the steps and ramps between the shelters – which used fresh-looking pink bricks of a type made by the London Brick Company between 1936 and c.1957. Also, the steel ring in the centre of the platform bears an eroded inscription which matches that on another ring at Weymouth, where the inscription can clearly be read as 'CM523, Sir Wm A & Co Ltd, 1939'. There can be no doubt, then: Monkhams Hall was reused as an anti-aircraft gun site during the Second World War.

To confuse matters further, there appear to have been yet later modifications to turn the former gun platform into some sort of garden feature, with an open drain cut into the concrete surface, a series of radially aligned brick supports and paving slabs around the outer edge, and four large holes, equally spaced around the central ring, smashed into the concrete. There are two layers of concrete, moreover: the Second World War gun-mounting is set into the first of these, but at some point another had been laid over the top.

A detailed shot of the gun ring which lay in the centre of Structure A.
(Nadia Durrani for GWAG)

A close-up of the gun ring bearing an eroded inscription that matches that
on another ring at Weymouth, where the inscription can clearly be read as
'CM523, Sir Wm A & Co Ltd, 1939'. There can be no doubt that Monkhams
Hall was reused as an anti-aircraft gun site during the Second World War.
(Nadia Durrani for GWAG)

GWAG member Odette Nelson excavates a trench just outside Structure A. The items found there, including rough clinker associated with an oven – presumably for making tea or to keep warm – paint an evocative picture of the lives of the soldiers once based here. (Nadia Durrani for GWAG)

In the trench on the north-west side of the platform we also exposed a layer of broken-up concrete just beneath the grass, with a layer of fine clinker beneath. It was impossible to date these deposits, though we found two more corkscrew barbed-wire supports, and a possible stove-pipe hole in the concrete roof of the western shelter may imply that the clinker derived from a wartime stove inside.

The picture elsewhere on the site was equally confused by Second World War modifications and garden features, the latter apparently dating variously from before, between and after the wars. Rubble-clogged and heavily overgrown, 'Structure D' (as we dubbed it) comprised a rectangular building of 12.9m x 6.7m formed of a low brick wall. Fred Nash, the Military Archaeologist at Essex County Council, had visited Monkhams and made a report on Structure D, reckoning it to be a Second World War barrack block. He had noted the Second World War-type 'fletton' bricks that formed the wall, and also the fact that the top bricks were laid on edge (as 'headers' rather than 'stretchers'), as if they had supported a wooden or corrugated-iron superstructure.

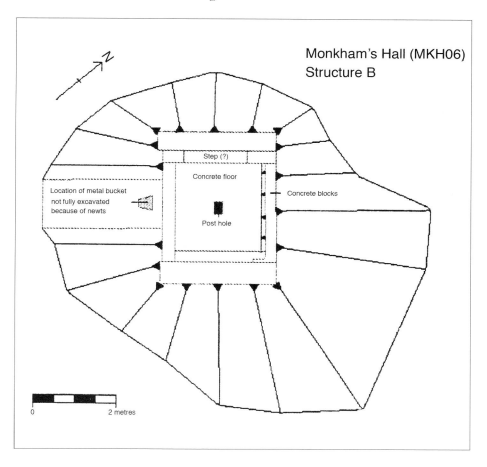

Plan of the Monkhams Hall observation and sighting post – Structure B. (Fizz Altinoluk for GWAG)

The identification of Structure D as a barrack block is probably right, but it now seems likely that an existing building was modified – though not, as it happens, one of First World War vintage. Local knowledge had it that Structure D was a late Victorian greenhouse in the garden of Monkhams Hall, and GWAG members tested this idea by clearing a 1m-sq. area in a corner of the building. We revealed that the internal concrete floor stopped about 45cm short of the wall, leaving a gravel-filled soakaway – an obvious greenhouse feature. It was also clear that there was a wide gap in the wall on the (short) southern side of the building, which would have maximised sunlight coming through a presumed wood-and-glass superstructure. Moreover, it was evident on close examination of the mortar that two extra courses of bricks had been added to heighten the wall, and other changes were implied by the sheer quantity of brick rubble in and around the structure. So it *was* a greenhouse, but at some point it had been turned into something else. Our discovery of another corkscrew barbed-wire support strengthened Fred Nash's interpretation. But was this greenhouse also used in the First World War? Indeed, did it even exist at the time, or was local knowledge of its date defective? Use as a First World War barracks is certainly possible. Archive photographs of the nearby Pole Hill site clearly show barracks beside the gun emplacement. At present we do not know.

Structure C, on the other hand, seems likely to date from the first war. Local knowledge has it as a First World War ammo store or latrine. Site director David Thorpe cleared the feature of litter and vegetation to reveal a subterranean structure formed of poured concrete. Rectangular in shape, it had been divided into two equal-sized 'boxes' by a central wall, each box measuring just under 1m sq. The western box was cleared of 0.75m of rubble and slate, probably from a nearby house refurbishment, and horse dung. This revealed the remains of a rubble-choked iron cistern fed from a nearby spring through salt-glazed earthenware pipes. So it certainly was not an ammo store, and it seems too elaborate for a latrine. Presumably it was a water store, and, given its substantial construction and the similarity of its concrete to that forming the roofs of the shelters on the gun emplacement, it may date from the First World War.

Yet more significant was Structure B, which project director Neil Faulkner investigated. Clearance here revealed a low-walled structure formed of a cement screed floor and two courses of mortared concrete breeze blocks, with earth banks around the outside. The structure was 2m square, stood 0.45m high, and there may have been an entrance on the north-western side. The broken concrete blocks found in the rubble fill imply that the structure may originally have stood higher. The surrounding earth bank was approximately 2m in width, and an exploratory trench cut through it revealed it to have been formed mainly of clay with some iron debris (including a bucket); the absence of rubble from the structure in the mound makes it almost certain that the mound is contemporary with the structure and that it was built to stabilise, strengthen and protect the walls. The mound trench was dug only to a

GWAG co-director Neil Faulkner opens up 'Structure B' a low-walled, 2m-square building formed of a cement screed floor, two courses of mortared concrete breeze-blocks, and earth banks around the outside. But what was Structure B? (Nadia Durrani for GWAG)

As digging continued, we concluded that Structure B was probably an observation and sighting position serving the anti-aircraft gun. Note the central post-setting, with the remains of the squared post from within beside the hole. (Nadia Durrani for GWAG)

depth of about 0.30m because a colony of newts was found within it and the excavation was therefore terminated. In the centre of the cement screed floor was a 10cm-square posthole containing large quantities of decayed wood.

Structure B is only 6m away from the gun emplacement and is on exactly the same orientation, even having its probable access point on the north-western side. It seems highly likely that this was an observation and sighting position serving the gun. The concrete mix used in the breeze-blocks, like that in Structure C, looks very similar to that in the roofs of the shelters. Again, then, the possibility arises that this may be an original First World War feature.

Why is the dating so difficult? Only twenty-one years separated the First and Second World Wars. Many things changed little in that time. Even where they did change, how can you tell? Concrete mixes are not standardised. Bricks get recycled. Local building firms have their own ways of doing things. Some of the bricks used on parts of the gun emplacement and the remodelled greenhouse were post-First World

Structure B after clearance. The breeze blocks used in this structure resemble the concrete used elsewhere on the site, notably in the reinforced concrete roofs of the two brick shelters forming part of Structure A. It seems likely, on this basis, that Structure B was also established in the First World War. (Nadia Durrani for GWAG)

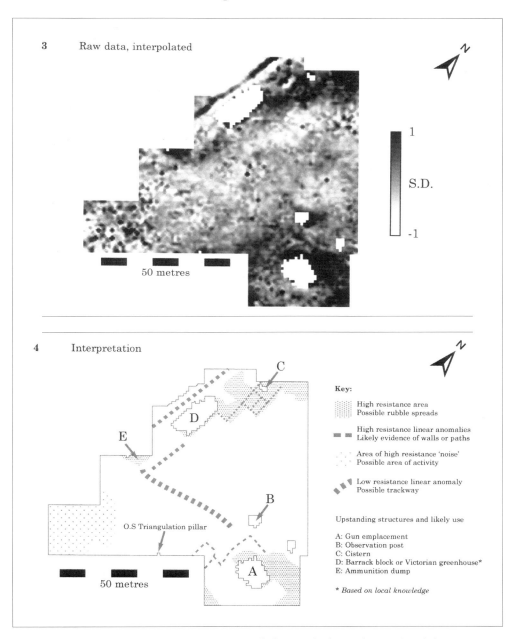

3   Raw data, interpolated

1

S.D.

-1

50 metres

4   Interpretation

C

D

E

B

O.S Triangulation pillar

A

50 metres

Key:

High resistance area
Possible rubble spreads

High resistance linear anomalies
Likely evidence of walls or paths

Area of high resistance 'noise'
Possible area of activity

Low resistance linear anomaly
Possible trackway

Upstanding structures and likely use

A: Gun emplacement
B: Observation post
C: Cistern
D: Barrack block or Victorian greenhouse*
E: Ammunition dump

* *Based on local knowledge*

Geophysical survey results for Monkhams Hall, showing both raw data (top) and the geophysicists' interpretation (bottom). (Dave Hibbitt and Angie Cannon for GWAG)

Structure C was excavated by GWAG co-director David Thorpe. Little did he know when he started that he would be digging a deep hole filled with building debris and horse dung. (Nadia Durrani for GWAG)

David Thorpe and Fizz Altinoluk busy excavating Structure C. (Angie Cannon)

A shot down into Structure C with the upper fill removed, revealing the concrete walls, the iron cistern at the base, and the salt-glazed feeder pipes. (Nadia Durrani for GWAG)

War, but not much else was datable. It is rare to find diagnostic artefacts in contexts that can be directly related to construction events. Had the newts nested elsewhere and the trench through the mound been dug further, Neil Faulkner might have found a coin, and if it were post-1918 it would have *proved* that the structure was not of the First World War. It was not to be.

A picture was emerging, but it was like a photograph that has been doubly or trebly exposed, with events at different times superimposed and not clearly distinguishable. The same problem confronted the geophysicists, who had completed their survey while the diggers were working on the gun emplacement, the observation post, the cistern, and the greenhouse-cum-possible-barrack-block. Several areas of high resistance had been recorded around the structures – perhaps spreads of rubble, areas of hard-standing, or even building foundations. There were also some strong linear features, perhaps buried walls or metalled paths, especially in the vicinity of the cistern and the greenhouse, as well as to the north-west of the gun emplacement. Possibly of greatest interest, however, was a low-resistance

GWAG co-director David Thorpe and industrial historian Jim Lewis discuss the interpretation of Structure E, a wide concrete platform revealed beneath a thin skim of rough turf. It is likely to have been an open-air ammunition dump. (Angie Cannon for GWAG)

linear anomaly extending from an area of high resistance on the north-western edge of the survey towards the gun emplacement. Could it be a track? Usually a track would be represented by higher resistance, but either the nature of the feature or local ground conditions might sometimes dictate otherwise. And what of the high-resistance area from which the 'track' extended? The diggers were already testing the ground.

Structure E – as it became – turned out to be a 10cm-thick concrete platform measuring 5m x 5.6m. There was no evidence at all of any superstructure, and the discovery of a corkscrew barbed-wire support *in situ* on the edge of the platform strongly implies that it was once surrounded by a barbed-wire fence. The most likely interpretation seems to be that it was an ammo-dump. A photograph of the anti-aircraft gun site at Pole Hill appears to show ammunition crates stacked in the open (see page 58). Structure E shares the alignment of the gun emplacement and the observation post, and appears to be linked with them by that possible track on the geofizz plot. Perhaps it was set well back to avoid the risk of accidental explosion due to sparks from the discharge of the gun. Could

GWAG geophysicists Angie Cannon and Dave Hibbitt carefully surveyed the entire site. (Dave Hibbitt for GWAG)

The photographer photographed. Nadia Durrani photographing Structure B for the GWAG archive. The outbuildings of Monkhams Hall can be seen in the background. (Angie Cannon)

it even be the case that the metal wheel found beside the gun emplacement had fallen off an ammunition trolley?

Time ran out at Monkhams. A small team of about eight spent five
solid days exploring the remains on the hill, but it was not enough to
disentangle the successive phases of first war, second war, and garden
use. Our knowledge of the layout and operation of an anti-aircraft gun
site from the First Blitz therefore remains hazy. Field research is planned
at other sites, and at one has already begun. This is One Tree Hill in
Southwark, a prominent hilltop location close to Central London with
clear views over the city, and one with no record of reuse in the Second
World War. The gun emplacement was recorded in late August 2007, and
evidence found for extensive concrete spreads nearby. The Great War
Archaeology Group is working with a group of local people actively
involved in caring for One Tree Hill, a small area of mainly wooded
land owned by the council and open for public use. The plan is to com-
bine further fieldwork with archive research and oral history. Though
for long a municipal park – the remains of which in places obscure the
'imprint' of the First World War archaeology – we hope that a clear picture of what happened on One Tree Hill between 1914 and 1918 will in
due course emerge.

7

Airfields and Fighters

Because anti-aircraft gun emplacements were numerous, relatively small, and located on high ground, a number of them survive and can be investigated. The handful of airfields from which London's home-defence fighters operated, by contrast, sprawled across the flat, low-lying land needed by post-war urban development. None of the four airfields in the Great War Archaeology Group's Lea Valley study area has escaped intact. Only limited areas of the original airfields were available for exploration on the two sites we tackled – Chingford and North Weald Bassett. Both interventions were quick 'evaluations'.

Once desktop research has been done, an evaluation is a field exercise designed to test 'archaeological potential'. Do any archaeological remains actually survive? Can you see any bits of upstanding building, any tell-tale humps and bumps, any mounds of overgrown rubble? Does geofizz reveal any sub-surface features – wall foundations, spreads of concrete, blocked-up cisterns? What do you find if you dig small trenches – is it just layers of soil and bits of modern rubbish, or do you come down onto archaeological features? The idea of an evaluation is to get a basic impression of what is there, how well preserved, and whether or not fuller investigation might be worthwhile.

No one, as far as we could tell, had ever dug an archaeological trench to find out what might survive on the site of a First World War airfield. We were determined, therefore, to evaluate the archaeological potential on the two sites where we discovered open ground and supportive land-owners. The airfields, after all, were crucial. The lights had exposed and tracked the raiders as they approached the capital. The guns had corralled

A view of the small area of pasture wedged between the King George and William Girling Reservoirs in the Lea Valley, Essex: all that remains of the First World War Royal Naval Air Service Airfield at Chingford. This view looks north. (Julian Evan-Hart for GWAG)

A selection of metal-detected finds from the Chingford site, confirming its identity as a former wartime airfield. (Julian Evan-Hart for GWAG)

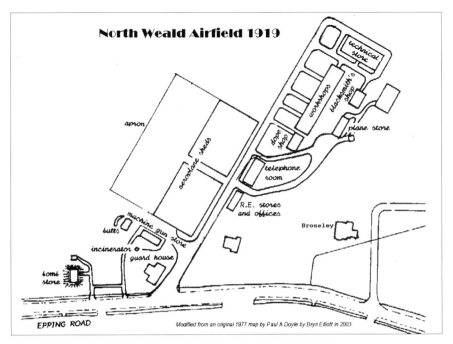

North Weald Airfield 1919

technical store

apron

workshops

blacksmith's shop

dope shop

plane store

aeroplane sheds

telephone room

R.E. stores and offices

Broseley

machine gun store

butts

incinerator

guard house

bomb store

EPPING ROAD

Modified from an original 1977 map by Paul A Doyle by Bryn Elliott in 2003

Comparison between plans of the First World War airfield and those of the later Second World War airfield at North Weald Bassett revealed areas currently under grass that did not appear to have been built on after 1918. GWAG was able to dig test-pits both on the site of the former workshops and on the south-east edge of the former aircraft hangars. (North is to the top of the plan and the scale is approximately 1:2000.) (Courtesy of Bryn Elliott and the Ad Astra House Museum)

them into the skies above the city limits. But it was fighters that had turned these skies into a killing zone.

The First World War airfields were operated by both the Royal Naval Air Service and the Royal Flying Corps, respectively part of the Navy and the Army (it was not until April 1918 that the RNAS and the RFC were combined to form the Royal Air Force). Most of the airfields established in the early part of the war were for training purposes, and only slowly during 1915 and 1916 did airfields and associated fighter squadrons emerge that were dedicated to home defence. The problem was partly uncertainty about how best to meet the Zeppelin threat: strategic bombing was new, and argument continued through 1915 about whether guns or planes were the best defence. The problem was also lack of aircraft and trained pilots given the relentless demands of attritional warfare on the Western Front.

A small team at work test-pitting in early 2006 on the site of the 1916–18 aircraft workshops of 39 Home Defence Squadron at North Weald Bassett Airfield. (Ali Baldry for GWAG)

Jim Lewis, GWAG's industrial historian, discovered that a 150-acre site in the Lea Valley at Chingford, bordered to the north by the King George Reservoir, had been opened as an RNAS airfield in 1915. It was listed as a 'second class landing-ground', not least because the clay soil on which it was built was poorly draining, causing problems in wet weather. Take-off and landing could be hazardous (and it is worth recalling that more pilots were killed in accidents than in combat). On the other hand, in the airfield's favour was the large reservoir to the north, a highly visible landmark for returning pilots. The airfield was controlled by 49 Wing, and was used both for training and as a base for 44 Squadron, which was dedicated to home defence.

Jim tracked down a photograph of Chingford Airfield taken in 1915 (see page 60). It shows a long row of substantial, single-storey, gable-roofed huts; they appear to be timber, though painted white, on low brick or concrete foundations. In front of the huts the grass landing-ground can be seen, and several different types of aircraft. The whole thing looks pretty rough-and-ready – something improvised quickly to plug the huge gaps in Britain's home defences. What, if anything, would survive on the site?

Aeroplane Twin-shed

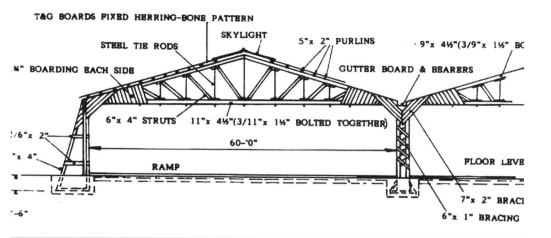

A plan dated 1918 showing the design in cross-section of an aeroplane twin-shed of the kind depicted in contemporary photographs of North Weald Bassett Airfield. Would the footings survive below ground? (Courtesy of Bryn Elliott and the Ad Astra House Museum)

In January 2006 a team of six diggers spent a day on the site. Four-fifths of the First World War airfield, which was given up in 1919, has disappeared in the construction of the William Girling Reservoir, which lies immediately south of the older King George Reservoir. All that now remains is a roughly triangular area of grassland wedged between the old reservoir to the north and new to the south. The ground is owned by Thames Water and let out as sheep pasture. Both the water engineers and the tenant farmer were interested and supportive. Contractors working nearby had brought up large quantities of building and industrial debris of probable early twentieth-century date – we could see it in their spoil – when constructing an approach road for equipment along the northern edge of the field. Elsewhere, unevenness in the ground implied buried features or dumps, and odd lumps of material were visible on the surface here and there. It seemed likely, therefore, that airfield archaeology would survive beneath the turf on the undisturbed pasture. There was, after all, no evidence that anything significant had happened on the site since 1919. Jim's photograph seemed to show airfield buildings along the edge of the field; with luck, most of what the reservoir had cut away would be

A test-trench on the presumed site of the footings of a First World War aircraft hangar at North Weald Bassett revealed a clay-packed slot for a timber ground-beam, along with a tell-tale scatter of nails and roofing tacks. (Ali Baldry for GWAG)

just the grass take-off and landing area. Test-pits were called for, targeting the areas of uneven ground.

Both historical research and local memory contributed to our picture of what we were looking for. A First World War airfield might be expected to have wooden hangars for the aircraft; a headquarters and communications centre; barracks for both air and ground crew; separate messes for officers, NCOs and other ranks; workshops; storage facilities, including fuel and ammo stores; and such things as latrines and field drains. On the other hand, we could expect many of the structures to be simply, even flimsily constructed, reflecting wartime haste and improvisation.

Two test-pits, spaced 15m apart, failed to locate the presumed 'western range' of airfield buildings. Beneath the topsoil there was a thin spread of scraggy gravel and then what appeared to be the natural clay. The more diagnostic among the finds – which included bits of metal, broken glass, potsherds, oyster and whelk shell, fragments of ceramic tile, an iron spike, a piece of lead piping, a lump of concrete – pointed to an early twentieth-century date.

Two other test-pits dug along the presumed 'northern range' were more productive. Though one produced only brick rubble, fragments of broken flagstone, and virtually no finds, it was clear from the material that there must have been a building very close by. Test-pit 1 was better still. Located on the edge of a slight hump, we hoped that it might be placed so as to clip the eastern edge of a building. The 2m x 1m test-pit revealed a layer of loose gravel containing iron slag, clinker and coke, which we interpreted as a levelling layer following the abandonment of the airfield in 1919. Beneath was a substantial demolition deposit formed of flagstones, red and yellow bricks, chunks of yellow mortar, and broken glass. Some of the flagstones looked as if they might be roughly *in situ*.

The bricks were typical of those used in late nineteenth and early twentieth-century buildings. Some of them were bitumened, which is characteristic of military brickwork during the world wars. On some of the bricks, moreover, there was a ghosting of wooden supports impressed into the bitumen, implying that the building had comprised a brick-work foundation with a wooden superstructure – something typical of military buildings of the period, and exactly what appeared to be shown in Jim's photograph. At the end, presumably, the wood had been salvaged for reuse, but the brick had been left as not worth the effort of carrying away.

The following April Julian Evan-Hart carried out a quick metal-detector scan of the site. He recovered several diagnostic artefacts: bits of copper, aluminium and steel that had perhaps been parts of aircraft instruments or repair patches. At the same time as the metal-detector scan, Angie Cannon and Dave Hibbitt carried out some geophysics. Alas, the presence of huge industrial pylons running across one end of the site made a magnetic survey impossible. Moreover, the ground-based electrical interference from these pylons, the nearby factories and also an electrical sub-station rendered the resistance survey results useless. This was not, as Dave said, a good site for geophysics.

Chingford had been a successful evaluation: no evidence of later reuse of the site to cloud the picture, and good reason for thinking that the footprint of some of the airfield buildings, especially on the northern range, survives beneath a modest depth of topsoil and levelled demolition debris.

North Weald Bassett was a different proposition. This airfield lies just beyond the north-eastern sprawl of Greater London. It began life as a Royal Flying Club airfield, and was taken over by the war effort only in August 1916, when it joined Hainault Farm and Suttons Farm as one of three Essex airfields used by 39 Squadron – the unit of Royal Flying Corps night-fighters that became the elite of home defence. The airfield was disused from 1919, but was then reconstructed in 1926, and eventually played a major role in the Battle of Britain. It continued in use after the Second World War, and is still used today by light aircraft. Unlike Chingford, moreover, which lies forgotten, the history of North Weald Airfield has been meticulously catalogued by enthusiasts like former police helicopter pilot Bryn Elliott and others associated with the Ad Astra House Air Museum. Bryn was able to supply a sheaf of plans and photographs of different dates, including plans from 1916–19 showing the layout of the First World War airfield.

All surface trace of First World War buildings has disappeared. The north-western half of the site, where a 1919 plan shows the First World War aircraft hangars, is now occupied by larger, brick-built hangars of Second World War date, which are still used by various small businesses. The south-eastern half, where other airfield buildings were located, is dominated by the car park of Booker's Cash and Carry. However, careful comparison of plans showing successive building phases, coupled with examination of the actual ground, appeared to show that the footings of former First World War buildings might lie beneath areas of grass verge. Two areas looked to have real potential. Area A – as we called it –

comprised a grass verge on the north-western side of Booker's car park, just inside their outer fence, where the contemporary plans showed workshops and yards during the First World War. Area B comprised another grass verge, this time behind the back wall of the Second World War hangars, since the plans implied that the original hangars had extended somewhat further to the south-east.

A team of seven dug a total of five test-pits. Four of these were placed along the presumed line of workshops and yards in Area A. Test-pit 1 revealed a possible surface formed of compacted pebble-and-clay with large fragments of charcoal and other industrial waste. Demolition debris – concrete, brick, asbestos roofing, fragments of glass, a fragment of glazed tile – implied a lost building. Both here and in two of the other three test-pits, finds of workshop-type debris were also abundant, with numerous bits of metalwork, including aluminium sheeting, copper and lead tubing, a copper electrical joint with attached wire, and various other bits of metalwork which may represent aircraft parts. Only test-pit 4 was a dud: dug into a low mound, it revealed a modern dump, possibly from the building of Booker's Cash and Carry. The best find was a fired cartridge case of probable First World War date. The combination of at least one surface, much demolition debris, varied metal waste, and the cartridge make it likely that we had located the workshops and yards depicted on contemporary plans of the First World War airfield.

In Area B, where the aircraft hangars were suspected, we dug just one 1m x 3.5m trench extending outwards from close to the rear wall of the standing Second World War buildings. The outer, south-eastern extent of the trench was undisturbed ground: here, the loose, loamy, mid-brown topsoil proved to be relatively deep. The inner extent of the trench revealed something quite different, however. Immediately beneath the topsoil and extending across the width of the trench – running parallel, therefore, with the brick wall of the Second World War hangar – were two wide bands of yellow clay separated by a band of loam approximately 0.75m wide. The latter looked like the 'fill' of a cut into the clay. But the clay itself could not be natural, since it ended abruptly halfway across the trench. Excavation of part of the fill showed it to have a depth of only 7cm, beneath which lay a flat base formed of more yellow clay. But bands of mid-brown clay could also be seen, proving beyond doubt that the yellow clay was not a natural deposit but had been deliberately laid down. We cannot be certain, but all the evidence – the location, the orientation, the width and depth of the 'slot' defined by the yellow clay – points to this being the footing of the First World War aircraft hangar shown on the plans.

The evidence fitted in other ways, too. Photographs of 1917 and 1918 vintage, and a construction diagram for a hangar dated 1918, show wholly timber structures, reinforced with ground-fast exterior bracing. And we can assume that airfield buildings were thrown up fast; they were temporary structures, built for the duration only, so there was no value in digging deep foundations. The faint archaeological imprint in the trench seemed right. So did the scatter of nails, bolts, washers, roofing tacks, and other miscellaneous metalwork in the topsoil and the fill of the slot – much of it, presumably, derived from the construction or demolition of the wooden hangar.

The North Weald evaluation, like that at Chingford, had proved the survival of First Blitz archaeology, and the potential for further investigation.

A forgotten relic of the First Blitz. Still standing a few miles from North Weald Bassett, in the village of Moreton, is this wooden aircraft hangar, moved to this site to be used first as a barn, later as a garage. It is now at risk. Will it be rescued? (Ali Baldry for GWAG)

The interior roof structure of the Moreton aircraft hangar corresponds exactly to that shown on the 1918 plan. How common are such buildings? How many have survived? (Ali Baldry for GWAG)

A final surprise was in store. Bryn Elliott alerted the GWAG team to the survival at nearby Moreton village of one of the original wooden hangars from North Weald Airfield. It had been transported to the site for use as a farm barn at some point between 1919 and 1922, and has served as a garage in more recent times. Now disused, it remains essentially intact, though dilapidated. However, the land on which it stands is up for sale, so that the hangar is now under threat from developers ever pushing the boundaries of the London conurbation further into the surrounding countryside. How many of these 'flat-pack' aircraft hangars of the First Blitz survive elsewhere? How many people are aware that this old barn, sides bulging, roof gaping, once housed the night-fighting 'Zepp killers' of 39 Squadron? Let us hope that the building, a minor monument to the First Blitz, can somehow be saved, perhaps by taking it down, moving it to a place where it can be cared for, and there reconstructing it.

8

The Crash Site

When Julian Evan-Hart's metal-detecting team surveyed Crofts Field at Theberton Hall Farm on 14 April 2006 looking for the remains of L48, it was not the first Zeppelin crash site they had visited. Back in January, on a bitterly cold but bright Sunday morning, seven detectorists and four archaeologists had been on site at Oakmere Park in Potters Bar, just north of London. This was where airship ace Heinrich Mathy's L31 had been shot down on the night of 1–2 October 1916. It was one of two Zeppelins – the other being SL11 at nearby Cuffley – brought down in the Great War Archaeology Group's Lea Valley study area. It is no coincidence that two of the five Zeppelin crash sites in Britain are in this area: it was the main approach corridor of airships making for the capital, so it was here that the decisive battle for air supremacy was fought, here that the British home defence created a primary killing zone.

We had decided at the outset that we wanted to investigate at least one of the crash sites. Many Second World War aircraft crashes have been excavated, though usually by enthusiastic hobbyists rather than professional archaeologists. Julian Evan-Hart is, in fact, one of the most experienced aviation crash site investigators in the country, and it was because of this that the GWAG directors had first made contact with him. But even Julian had never dug a Zeppelin. No one had. In archaeological terms, this was *terra incognita*. What would remain? What would the archaeological imprint be on the ground – or rather, under the ground – of an aerial combat fought 10,000ft up ninety years ago? And what, if anything, might be learned from uncovering the wreckage?

Crofts Field, Theberton Hall Farm, Suffolk, June 2006: the first ever archaeological excavation of a Zeppelin crash site begins. Time was of the essence: the dig needed to be completed in three days (due partly to television funding and film schedules). Thus the mechanical digger begins to shift earth on the D-shaped field. What of L48 would remain? (Nadia Durrani for GWAG)

We visited both the Cuffley and the Potters Bar sites. Most of the Cuffley site is covered by mid-twentieth-century housing. In any case, the Cuffley airship was not strictly a Zeppelin at all, but a Schütte-Lanz – a type of airship made by a rival company with a wooden rather than a duralumin frame – and the concern was that comparatively little would have survived the fire. Potters Bar looked more promising. Contemporary photographs showed much of the wreckage of Mathy's Zeppelin piled up against an oak tree (subsequently dubbed 'the Zeppelin Oak'), and though the tree has now gone – its broken and twisted branches having succumbed to the saw when they were deemed hazardous at some point in the 1960s – its former location is precisely known. It stood at what is now the entrance to a private housing development in a suburban street called Tempest Avenue. The street post-dates the First World War, and it was named in honour of Wulstan Tempest, the 39 Home Defence

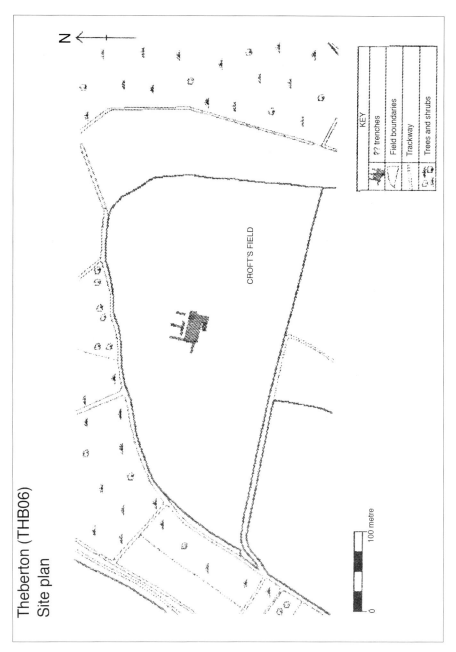

Plan showing the full extent of excavated trench within Crofts Field at Theberton Hall
Farm. (Fizz Altinoluk for GWAG)

Having mechanically removed a substantial amount of top-soil, the archaeologists and detectorists line up to begin scouring the freshly exposed surface for clues. (Nadia Durrani for GWAG)

Squadron pilot who shot down L31. Behind the houses and gardens of Tempest Avenue lies Oakmere Park, an extensive area of open land with lawns, lakes and leisure facilities, owned and maintained by Hertsmere District Council. Here was a piece of ground we might explore.

We were told stories by local historians about bits of Zeppelin being found in the 1960s when the oak tree was cut down and again when the lakes in the park were dredged. So there was stuff – or there had been – and our aim was to find out how much was still left in the ground, and whether there was any patterning in the distribution of debris; in particular, whether or not we had concentrations of material representing one or more impact points. The model for what to expect was the Second World War aircraft crash. Typically, the more vulnerable parts of the superstructure, especially the wings and the tail-plane, sometimes broke away and contributed to a spread of debris, often over a large area. But the fuselage usually smashed into the ground at high speed, exploding as

A view looking west – taken from the roof of the GWAG Landrover – shows the dimensions of the excavation area, which covered the metal-detected 'impact zone'. A group of archaeologists can be seen digging a sondage to test whether or not the curving lines and blotches on the freshly exposed surface were natural. (Nadia Durrani for GWAG)

it did so, with heavy engine components often burrowing deeply into the subsoil, pulling other parts of the plane with them, reaching depths of up to 5m. Such impact points or entry holes are represented in aviation archaeology by a blast-pit filled with twisted metal fragments and blackened by aviation fuel, lubricating oil, corroded aluminium, and the burning of combustible fragments – or, on the surface, in metal-detector survey, by a concentration of debris within a wider scatter. What Julian was really looking for at Oakmere Park was one or more of the places where one or other of L31's six engines – the only really heavy elements on the airship – had hit the ground.

The investigation had begun back in May 2005, when, with support from Hertsmere Council, and advice from the Potters Bar and District Historical Society, an excavation team had dug three small test-pits in the park. However, despite strenuous hand-digging through clay, sand and gravel to a depth of almost half a metre, and despite numerous finds

Metal-detectorists Julian Evan-Hart and Martin Plummer detect over the freshly exposed surface. Martin (right) is using a 'hoard hunter' – a high-powered metal-detector capable of locating large metal objects like engine components at depth. (The BBC television crew is in the background on the left.) (Nadia Durrani for GWAG)

of random modern rubbish, not a single fragment of Zeppelin had been recovered. Nor were any of the seven local residents who were in when we knocked at houses in nearby Chase Avenue able to report ever having found any strips of shiny lightweight metal digging in their gardens.

Then, towards the end of the day, the occupant of No. 12 Chase Avenue, who had just returned home, came across to the park to see what the diggers there were up to. She reported that her front drive had been paved just two weeks before – and that when they removed the garden soil overlying the clay subsoil they had found plenty of 'folded, lightweight metal', which 'looked like chewing-gum wrapper, silver on both sides, that had been folded up tight.' There was a stunned silence around the trench. Then someone said, 'Where is it?'

Some of the soil had been taken to a local primary school and sieved, all of the children recovering lots of the lightweight metal. And then? And then it had all been put in the skip.

Metal-detectorist Martin Plummer studies a find from the plough-soil as a new area is machine-stripped. (Nadia Durrani for GWAG)

The coincidence was too much: surely these had been fragments of the Zeppelin airframe? The driveway of No. 12 was now fully paved over and inaccessible, and though we dug three small holes in the rear garden and on the grass verge in front of the house, we found nothing. Presumably there had been a localised concentration of debris in one particular spot, found by chance a couple of weeks before, when there was no one on hand to explain that the children were not handling any old metal fragments but the scant remains of a First World War German airship shot down ninety years before.

So the following January we returned to the site, this time with Julian Evan-Hart's metal-detecting team. The detectorists walked in a line slowly southwards from the northern boundary of the park, listening for signals in their headphones as they swung their machines gently to and fro in front of them. Occasionally one would stop to dig out a find with his miniature spade, and one of the archaeologists would be on hand to record the exact find-spot. There were numerous coins, the earliest a worn George II halfpenny, some modern cutlery, one or two dinky toys, a dog's identity tag, and an Auxiliary Fire Service cap badge (of probable Second World War date). But at first there was nothing that could be associated with a Zeppelin. The soil was sandy and acidic, and some of the finds, even coins no older than the 1950s, were coming up corroded and patinated. Was it possible that whatever fragments of L31 had remained after the site clearance in 1916 had now crumbled to nothing? Or were they buried more deeply? Most of the finds were recent, and even the 1950s coins were coming from up to 8in down.

Then, towards the end of the five-hour survey, one of the detectorists recovered a small section of aluminium covered in a blue powder. Almost immediately, right next to it, a corroded aluminium fabric grommet was found. Finally, a few feet further on, a twisted and corroded section of aluminium airframe appeared. But that was all.

We knew there had been a major concentration of debris around the Zeppelin Oak, a site now under tarmac, but known from contemporary

Digging with care: archaeologists and volunteers explore a section of the crash site. (Nadia Durrani for GWAG)

accounts and photographs. We had evidence for a probable secondary concentration in front of No. 12 Chase Avenue, a site now paved over. But our test-pits in the park had revealed nothing, and our metal-detector survey just three small fragments. The likelihood was that if anything substantial still remained in the ground it would lie, as at Cuffley, under the roads, houses and patios of suburban streets.

That was why, three months after the survey at Oakmere Park, Julian's team was at Theberton – a rural site, under the plough, accessible in its entirety. When Crofts Field yielded dozens of Zeppelin fragments in a tight concentration, the decision was taken to carry out a full-scale investigation. The landowners gave their permission. The tenant farmer, owner of what was, by the early summer, a ripening crop of barley in the field, also gave permission in return for adequate compensation for crop damage. The BBC, keen to film a full Zeppelin crash site investigation, funded the excavation, paying for diggers' accommodation, heavy machinery to cut the trenches, and the agricultural compensation.

The debris concentration detected in April had corresponded closely with the impression gained from contemporary air photographs of the location of the wreckage within the field. But the hedge that had subdivided the field in 1917, close to which the wreckage had lain, was no longer there; and the barley crop had grown to full height in the two months since the detector survey. Relocating the spot took time. This was done by a small team of seven archaeologists and detectorists working ahead of the full excavation team to assess how best to tackle the site. They observed a line of slightly stronger growth – higher and greener – running down the field: the grubbed-out hedge had created a crop mark. Following the line to about the halfway point across the field, the detecting equipment was then used to redefine the concentration. There was an inner zone of dense debris about 25m across, and an outer zone of slight scatter beyond. The size of the inner zone matched the diameter of an airship, making it highly likely that this was the precise point where L48 had come to ground, folding up on itself lengthways, like a concertina, leaving its nose-cone projecting into the air at an angle: in short, the impact zone.

The plough-soil represented a layer of severe disturbance, in which airship fragments were likely to have been damaged and shattered by machinery, and corroded by contact with air, surface water, and agrochemicals. We wanted to see beneath the plough-soil, where larger chunks of crash debris may have lain undisturbed for ninety years, and where we hoped to see a primary impact point. The rear engines had dragged the flaming mass of L48's superstructure down through the sky. If they had impacted with sufficient force, they were likely to have penetrated deeply into the ground, and we might expect a large pit, blackened with burning, grease and oil, and containing substantial fragments missed by the First World War salvage teams.

We hired a small digger to excavate a trial trench across the impact zone, but when it began work it was soon apparent that it was inadequate. Both tracks and bucket slipped helplessly on the flattened barley crop; the machine was too light to get proper purchase. A bigger machine was essential, but it would not be available from the local Tobin plant hire firm for several days. The main excavation was rescheduled accordingly: we would return with a full team for a three-day investigation starting on 26 June.

For everyone who took part, those three days were special. The sun shone most of the time. The golden barley contrasted with the lush green of the woods at the bottom of the field and the clear blue skies above. There were specks of red amid the gold: poppies, icons of modern war, were reminders that we had come to excavate a battlefield, and that sixteen men had died here. The whole GWAG team was on site, but this time with half a dozen archaeology students to help shift dirt, and half a dozen detectorists to ensure that every tiny fragment was recovered from the spoil. Field archaeology is sometimes rather ghettoised, with academic research, rescue excavation, and local society digs separate. Above all, the world of 'proper' archaeology rarely overlaps with that of metal-detecting and aviation crash site investigation. But here was a new kind of archaeology – the archaeology of modern conflict – that of necessity was forging rich new partnerships. The Theberton team was a mix of academics, professional diggers, amateur excavators, archaeology students, metal-detectorists, and aviation enthusiasts. All added valuable expertise and experience to the mix.

Also on site was the BBC television crew – producer-director John Hayes-Fisher along with his assistant producer, cameraman, soundman, and production manager. Filming always puts an extra charge of excitement and energy through a digging team. Visits by experts during the three days had the same effect. Ray Rimell, the leading British expert on Zeppelins was there, as was Simon Parry, a top aviation archaeologist, and

Military historian Ray Rimell (right) and aviation archaeologist Simon Parry, both visitors to the site, look across at the work under way. (Nadia Durrani for GWAG)

Guy Smith, a high-tech wizard involved in a pioneering Western Front trench-map project. The local media also turned up. There were double-page spreads in local papers, news reports on local radio, and site director David Thorpe reported live from the site on local television news.

Veteran Suffolk digger-driver Mick Loades drove his machine across the barley early on the morning of Monday 26 June, followed by a line of helmeted archaeologists laden with metal-detectors and geofizz machines, mattocks and shovels, toolboxes and gizmos. We first cleared the crop from the impact zone and then dug an initial trench about 20m long and 2.5m wide down the eastern side of this area. Subsequently, three more trenches of similar size were dug at right-angles to the first, extending east to west across the impact zone, and spaced 2.5m apart.

The plough-soil, a brown sandy loam, was around 30cm deep, and Mick was asked to remove all of this and to cut into the underlying sub-soil up to 10cm, in order to get well below all the plough ruts and give the excavation team a completely clean surface on which to work. With a good driver and a toothless bucket, features can show up exceptionally

The Theberton dig is filmed for a BBC2 *Timewatch* documentary *The First Blitz*. (Nadia Durrani for GWAG)

Field director David Thorpe talks archaeology with television director John Hayes Fisher – as part of a BBC2 *Timewatch* documentary. (Nadia Durrani for GWAG)

David Thorpe is broadcast live across East Anglia from the excavation site. Local interest was high and media coverage intensive. The First World War is a fundamental conflict for modern Europeans, and the excavation of what was, in effect, a battle site of that war in a Suffolk field was irresistibly newsworthy. (Nadia Durrani for GWAG)

well on a freshly machined surface. At Theberton, however, visibility was obscured by a dull orange subsoil formed of fluvio-glacial clays, sands and gravels, with occasional pebbles and chalk lumps. This sort of drift geology covers much of East Anglia, accounting for extensive areas of woodland, heath and rough pasture, or arable of only marginal value. These deposits were laid down by the dynamic water systems formed by melting glaciers at the end of the great Anglian Ice Age. Instead of dumping uniform layers across the whole surface, the glacial streams sorted material by size and weight, creating a geology of blotches and curving lines that can easily be mistaken for postholes and ditches.

The magnetometer and the metal-detectors, including a deep-penetration 'hoard hunter', were vital tools. Run repeatedly over the new surfaces exposed and over the spoil removed, they revealed that the eastern strip was largely sterile. Zeppelin debris was present in some quantity in the plough-soil dumped on the side of the trench, but there was almost none in the subsoil beneath, and certainly no blackened pit with abundant fragments representing an impact point.

The GWAG Landrover provides a new camera-angle during the Timewatch filming.
(Nadia Durrani for GWAG)

It was then that we decided to dig a series of parallel strips at right-angles to the first. The quantity of debris increased towards the south, and eventually the intervening baulks were removed and trenches 2, 3 and 4 were consolidated into a single, large, roughly square excavation by the end of the first day. Still there was no impact point: all of the finds were coming from the plough-soil or the uppermost, disturbed level of the subsoil; there was nothing at depth.

But there had to be an impact point. Twenty-five tons of machinery had dropped out of the sky from a height of 11,000ft and smashed into ground at this precise spot in the early hours of 17 June 1917. On the second and third days we tried every conceivable method to locate an impact point. Mick used his digger to extend the existing trench to encompass the full width of the debris concentration found by the detector survey. He also excavated long, single-bucket-width transects out from the impact zone, against the possibility that the plough-soil concentration was distorting the sub-surface picture, and that the impact point lay at one edge or even beyond it. Altogether,

GWAG geophysicist Dave Hibbitt 'geofizzing' a machine-stripped section of the 'impact zone' in Crofts Field. (Nadia Durrani for GWAG)

around 690 square metres of subsoil were exposed at the centre of the field.

Dave Hibbitt and Angie Cannon checked the measurements across the field, and ran their magnetometer around the northern and eastern margins of the impact zone in the hope of hitting major magnetic 'anomalies': nothing. Guy Smith used a hand-held GPS (global positioning system) unit to locate a position on the ground identified through computer-aided overlaying of contemporary air-photographic evidence onto a modern OS map. His calculations prompted an extension of the existing trench by around 5m on the southern side. The plough-soil was indeed rich in finds, and embedded in the upper subsoil was a small area of discoloration with lumps of aluminium alloy and the distinctive blue powdery traces of aluminium corrosion. With a little scraping they disappeared, and detectors run over the ground afterwards gave no further signals.

Sometimes, even after decades of ploughing, buried features leave slight undulations in the ground. Might the crater from which heavy components had been extracted by the First World War salvage teams have left some surface trace? Using a dumpy level, we measured the

Dave Hibbitt and Angie Cannon, the GWAG 'geofizz' team, at work. (Nadia Durrani for GWAG)

height of the land at 2m intervals along a 60m north-south transect just beyond the eastern edge of the excavation: nothing showed except the slight dropping away of the land towards the north and the unevenness of the plough rutting.

All these investigations merely confirmed the results of the metal-detector survey. Julian's team had correctly located the impact zone. Our main trench was in the right place. This trench had been machine-excavated to just below the base of the plough-soil, and had then been further shovel-cleaned, repeatedly scanned by metal-detector, and in places tested by the excavation of small sondages to make absolutely certain that all those blotches of clay and curves of sand really were natural. Across the whole area, evidence of disturbance was minimal and confined to the uppermost level – a superficial dusting of tiny pieces of charcoal, smears of blue powder, and the occasional aluminium or copper fragment. There were no entry holes or salvage pits, no concentrated mass of burning, aluminium oxide, oil staining, and metal debris. The only significant *in situ* archaeological feature was that formed by the grubbing out of the hedge across the middle of the field.

The metal-detectors recovered 329 small fragments of L48 from Crofts Field during the three-day excavation. There was a steel rod, probably from an engine, a short steel section with a nut at either end, and eight other unidentifiable steel fragments. There were fifty-four pieces of aluminium from the airframe or one or other of the gondolas, fifteen long aluminium rivets, six aluminium rivet heads, two large aluminium grommets, and a small aluminium grommet. There were also 182 pieces of once-molten or oxidised aluminium. There were two sections of copper-alloy tubing, a small folded copper-alloy joint, a small copper-alloy electrical component, four domed copper-alloy fasteners, and forty-five copper-alloy fabric eyelets. There were also six globules of lead, molten, oxidised, and originating from engine batteries. These must be added to the seventy similar fragments of L48 recovered in the April survey. Finally, there was another military button: in good condition, a copper-alloy cuff button from the uniform of an officer of the Imperial German Navy.

There was nothing of any size, however. The largest fragments of L48 we saw were two substantial sections of the aluminium airframe from elsewhere. One, somewhat corroded, is proudly displayed in a glass case in the porch of Theberton parish church. The other, in pristine condition, had been converted into an umbrella stand, purchased in a Brighton

David Thorpe holds up a piece of the L48 wreckage that was taken after the crash and turned into an umbrella stand – a wonderful example of what is commonly called 'trench art'. (Nadia Durrani for GWAG)

antique shop, and was brought to the site by a visitor to be admired as a superb example of First World War 'trench art'. Here were reminders of what had happened to L48. Whatever parts of it had not been removed by the official salvage teams – and where, one wonders, did all this material end up when the military scientists had finished with it? – had mostly been purloined by souvenir-hunters, who had scoured the site itself, and the farm tracks and country roads along which the debris had been moved. We had been left with only some 400 tiny fragments.

The BBC would have been happier had we recovered chunks of engine; and we, of course, as First World War archaeologists, would have enjoyed the thrill of finding and excavating them. But absence of evidence often tells its own story. Our search on Crofts Field had been exhaustive, and, while we could be certain from metal-detected finds in the plough-soil that we had located the impact zone, we could be equally certain that there was no entry-hole driven into the subsoil. Nor had there ever been, for even if the salvage teams had recovered every

The military had removed much of the L48 wreckage for investigation directly after the crash. As the previous image has illustrated, any significant parts that remained were removed by locals as keep-sake 'curiosities' or for onward sale. One large fragment is still proudly displayed in a glass case in the porch of the local parish church. (Nadia Durrani for GWAG)

fragment of buried metal, we would still have found the pit. Zeppelin L48's engines had not smashed into the ground at high speed, for their impact had failed to penetrate much deeper than around a foot.

If the impact was so slight, it is much easier to understand how three men had survived. A First World War airship crash was, it seems, very different from a Second World War aeroplane crash. Even as L48 fell 2 miles through the sky, residual hydrogen, the tattered fabric and buckling girders of the airframe, and of course the huge fire itself must have operated like a gigantic parachute, slowing the descent, breaking the fall, holding up the dead weight of the engines sagging beneath. Zeppelin L48, though parts of it became an inferno of burning gas and molten metal, half-floated down to earth, hitting the ground hard and crumpling up at the rear, but leaving the nose cone, the engines, and much else substantially intact and resting on the surface.

Conclusion

The strategic bombing pioneered in the skies over Britain between January 1915 and August 1918 was a new and terrible kind of war. In targeting industry, infrastructure and civilians, it aimed to destroy both the capacity and the will to resist. Although actual casualties and damage were light, especially compared with both the carnage elsewhere at the time, and with what was to come in later aerial bombing campaigns, it caused much fear, occasional panic, and widespread disruption, with blackouts, shutdowns and absenteeism. The construction of an effective home-defence system required the British to divert men, guns, aircraft and munitions from service elsewhere.

Strategic bombing was part of a revolution in war. It dissolved the distinction between the battlefield and the homeland. Battlefields were no longer distant, strange, even exotic places, where serried ranks of colourful warriors won military glory and built an empire. The bombers turned the homeland into a battlefield; they created a contested 'home front'. The new aerial techno-war made possible by science and industry meant that the military front line was no longer a secure defence of homes and hearths: the enemy could cross it, penetrate deeply beyond, and rain down death from the skies on women and children. Mass industrialised 'total' war had given rise to the 'total' battlefield, where no one was safe, everyone a target.

This new kind of war has left a distinctive archaeological imprint. Because of the distances over which the air war was fought, because of the speeds of the aircraft and their three-dimensional mobility, and because of the power and range of the weapons systems employed, conventional 'battlefield archaeology' cannot encompass it. Entire landscapes were militarised. The battlefield of a few miles morphed into a conflict landscape extending across hundreds of miles. The 'archaeology of combat' becomes, necessarily, an 'archaeology of conflict'. Perhaps, indeed, it should be wider still, an 'archaeology of confrontation', in which we see a continuity between 'hot wars' like 1914–18 and 1939–45, and the 'cold wars' of arms races and military deterrence that come before and after.

The archaeology of modern conflict is an infant sub-discipline that deals with a vast and almost untapped resource of material remains. The Council for British Archaeology's 1995–2002 *Defence of Britain Project* is an important partial exception. It represents the efforts of some 600 volunteers who recorded over 20,000 twentieth-century military sites in the United Kingdom. To do so they investigated local landscapes and catalogued historic monuments. However, of the 20,469 records on the *Defence of Britain Project* database, only 322 (1.6 per cent) are from the First World War, and only forty-four are airfields or other air-war installations; indeed, the database contains records for only six anti-aircraft guns and one searchlight of First World War date. By contrast, the First Blitz Project plotted thirty-three anti-aircraft gun emplacements and nineteen searchlight positions in its 40km x 40km study area alone. We have to conclude that the militarised landscapes of 1914–18 Britain are little known and poorly recorded.

Thousands of monuments survive, but most are forgotten, neglected, overgrown, crumbling away, vulnerable to destruction, outside any protective framework. This despite the fact that the First World War is an iconic event of huge and continuing global significance: the conflict that created much of the modern map of nation-states, and inaugurated the modern era of wars and revolutions. This conflict is now on the cusp of living memory. Almost all of the veterans are now dead. Soon almost all of the children of 1914–18 will also be dead. Within a decade or so, the First World War will have become deep history: it will no longer be part of our collective 'contemporary past', but part of a wholly historical past beyond the recall of any of us living.

The approaching centenary of the war will be a major focus for commemoration, research, re-evaluation, and public presentation. Archaeology, with its focus on the material remains of the conflict, all richly charged with memories and significances, should play a central

Crofts Field at Theberton, where sixteen German aircrew died in the wreckage of Zeppelin L48. The poppies provided the team with a clear reminded of why First World War archaeology matters. (Nadia Durrani for GWAG)

role in marking the anniversary. The Great War Archaeology Group favours a new national project – 'Britain at War, 1914–1918' – with an exclusive focus on recording, conserving and presenting the monuments of the First World War that survive in the British landscape, using a mix of archive research, oral history, and community-based archaeological fieldwork.

APPENDIX 1

Summary of First Blitz Project Fieldwork

OAKMERE PARK, POTTERS BAR,
HERTFORDSHIRE (TL 263 012)

L31 Zeppelin Crash Site

20 May 2005	Three test-pits	Negative results
29 January 2006	Metal-detector survey	Three finds attributable to L31, but no meaningful distribution

Conclusion: unlikely that any significant archaeological remains are accessible.

NORTH WEALD BASSETT AIRFIELD, NORTH
WEALD BASSETT, ESSEX (TL 488 046)

Royal Flying Corps Home-Defence Airfield

| 15 January 2006 | Four test-pits | Buried surfaces, demolition debris, industrial waste, and spent cartridge, indicating possible site of workshops |
| | One test-trench | Possible footings for timber aircraft hangar |

Conclusion: significant archaeological remains survive and are accessible in limited areas between later buildings.

WILLIAM GIRLING RESERVOIR, CHINGFORD
AND WOOD GREEN, ESSEX (TL 363 925)

Royal Naval Air Service Training and Home-Defence Airfield

28 January 2006	Four test-pits	Two revealed demolition debris likely to represent former airfield buildings
28 April 2006	Electrical-resistance survey	Unable to collect useful data
	Metal-detector survey	Finds included copper–alloy and aluminium objects definitely or probably attributable to aircraft

Conclusion: significant archaeological remains survive and are accessible in a small area of pasture between two large reservoirs.

THEBERTON HALL FARM, THEBERTON, SUFFOLK (TM 438 666)

L48 Zeppelin Crash Site

20 April 2006	Metal-detector survey	Numerous finds attributable to L48 forming tight concentration
21 June 2006	Metal-detector survey	Finds attributable to L48 redefining and confirming concentration
26–28 June 2006	Open-area excavation: whole metal-detector-defined 'impact zone' plus additional trial trenches machine-stripped and shovel-cleaned	No discernible archaeological features
	Magnetometer survey	No areas of high magnetic anomalies indicative of engine remains
	Metal-detector survey	Numerous finds attributable to L48, but all from plough-soil or upper surface of natural subsoil

Conclusion: no 'impact point' exists beneath modern plough-soil, implying slow descent and relatively soft landing for L48.

MONKHAMS HALL, WALTHAM ABBEY, ESSEX (TL 384 025)

Anti-Aircraft Gun Emplacement

25, 29–30 June 2006	Clearance and building recording	Five structures cleared and recorded: gun emplacement, observation post, cistern, green-house/barracks, and possible ammunition dump
	Electrical-resistance survey	Possible track between gun emplacement and ammunition dump plus vestiges of other possible structures identified
	Metal-detector survey	No diagnostic finds

Conclusion: significant archaeological remains survive relating to first war, second war, and garden use.

ONE TREE HILL, HONOR OAK PARK, SOUTHWARK, LONDON (TQ 354 742)

Anti-Aircraft Gun Emplacement

25–26 August 2007	Clearance and building recording	Gun emplacement
	Electrical-resistance survey	Areas of high resistance identified
	Seven test-pits	Revealed land consolidation, piped services, and possible First World War concrete surfaces

Conclusion: as well as gun emplacement, significant associated remains may survive as sub-surface features.

APPENDIX 2
First Blitz Project Personnel and Acknowledgements

THE AUTHORS

Dr Neil Faulkner is a Director of the Great War Archaeology Group (GWAG). He was educated at King's College, Cambridge, and the Institute of Archaeology, University College London (where he is now an Honorary Lecturer). He works as a freelance lecturer, editor, writer, excavator, and occasional broadcaster. He is Features Editor of the popular magazine *Current Archaeology*, and the author of numerous articles, academic papers, and several books, *The Decline and Fall of Roman Britain*, *Apocalypse: the great Jewish revolt against Rome, AD 66–73*, *Hidden Treasure: digging up Britain's past*, *The Sedgeford Hoard*, and *Rome: empire of the eagles*. He is also a Director of the Sedgeford Historical and Archaeological Research Project in north-west Norfolk, and of the Great Arab Revolt Project in southern Jordan. His television appearances include Channel Four's *Time Team*, BBC2's *Timewatch*, and Channel Five's *Revealed* series.

Dr Nadia Durrani has been involved in GWAG since its creation in 2005. She studied Archaeology and Anthropology at Cambridge, and took a PhD in Arabian Archaeology at University College London. She is Editor of Britain's best-selling world archaeology magazine, *Current World Archaeology*. She also edits and writes for a raft of books, magazines, and scholarly journals. She has previously published one book, about the archaeology of the western coast of Yemen, *The Tihamah Coastal Plain of South-West Arabia in its Regional Context, c.6000 BC–AD 600*. She has also worked for a range of archaeological programmes, including Channel Four's *Time Team*.

The chapters were based on text provided by members of the GWAG Team as follows:

CHAPTERS 1, 2 AND 8

Julian Evan-Hart has been involved in some 200 aircraft excavations and crash site searches. He has been a metal-detectorist since the 1980s. In 2003 he co-authored *The Beginners Guide to Metal Detecting*, while in 2006 he wrote the Hertfordshire volume for the *War Torn Skies* series. He has also translated a French book for the English market on *The Amiens Raid*, and writes regular metal-detecting articles for *Treasure Hunting* magazine and several historical magazines in the USA. Thanks are also due to Jules for additional fact-checking and editorial support throughout the book. Information for Chapter 1 also came from Ray Rimell's book, *The Last Flight of the L48*.

CHAPTER 4

Dr Jim Lewis is a retired electronics engineer and has spent most of his working life in the consumer electronics industry carrying out projects in many countries around the world. Since retirement he has had two books published on the industrial history of London's Lea Valley and another on the history of East Ham and West Ham. Jim is married with four grown-up sons. He currently lives in Grantham, where as a WEA tutor he teaches students with learning difficulties. Thanks are also due to Jim for his work with Dave Hibbitt on Chapter 5.

Chris Mackie is an archaeologist, broadcaster and writer. After a highly successful career in the RAF, he worked as an internal auditor in industry before moving on to manage a large National Trust property. Now retired from full-time work, he has been able to follow his passion for local history and archaeology, mainly in association with the Sedgeford Historical and Archaeology Research Project (SHARP), in which he has been deeply involved since its inception in 1996. More recently he has provided SHARP with a conduit for publicity through his expertise in dealing with all aspects of the press.

CHAPTER 5

David Hibbitt is the Director of Grantham Archaeology Group, a Director of Grid Nine Geophysics (www.gridnine-geophysics.co.uk), and a Practitioner of the Institute of Field Archaeologists. Although a keen digger, he has concentrated recently on non-intrusive investigations on numerous sites in the UK and abroad. He has been involved in television work with Channel Four, Channel Five and BBC2.

Angie Cannon has been interested in history and archaeology for many years. She gained her fieldwork experience with the Grantham Archaeology Group, and is now a Director of Grid Nine Geophysics. With thanks to Dave and Angie for additional fact-checking and editorial support throughout the book, for designing the maps, and for compiling Appendix 1.

CHAPTERS 6 AND 7

David Thorpe is a Director of GWAG. He is a professional digging archaeologist who has excavated in the US, Israel, Syria, Crete, Libya, Malaysia, Germany, China and Jordan, as well as in the City of London and on many other British sites. He currently directs the Copped Hall Trust Archaeological Project (excavating a Tudor mansion). His television appearances include Channel Four's *Time Team*, Channel Five's *Boudica's Treasures Revealed*, and BBC2's *Timewatch*.

Alison Baldry is a forensic archaeologist who has been involved in many of GWAG's excavations both as a digger and a photographer. She is a Scene of Crime Officer for Surrey Police.

Odette Nelson has been interested in archaeology since she was a small child living opposite the ruin of a once Nazi-owned house in Berlin. She has studied at Birkbeck College, University of London, and took her MA from the Institute of Archaeology, UCL.

OTHER ACKNOWLEDGEMENTS

Other GWAG members and volunteer excavators and metal-detectorists who worked on First Blitz Project sites include: Fizz Altinoluk, Elizabeth Bond, Don Cooper, Cat Edwards, Jeff Evans, Charlotte Elvidge, Jill Hooper, Gary Jordan, Gabe Moshenska, Martin Plummer, Rachel Quick, Dave Stuckey, Cliff Vickers and Duncan Ward.

The BBC2 *Timewatch* television crew who filmed at Theberton and Monkhams were John Hayes-Fisher (producer-director), Sarah Jobling (assistant producer), David Brill (cameraman), Paul Jenkins (soundman), and Chris Logan (production manager). The programme was commissioned and the fieldwork part-funded by John Farren, commissioning editor for *Timewatch*.

We are also grateful to all of the following, who either supplied information or images, or facilitated access to sites: Paul Adams, Booker's Cash and Carry; Bryn Elliott, Ad Astra House Air Museum; Keith French, Head Forest Keeper for the North of Epping Forest; Brian and Eleanor Hart, owners of Theberton Hall Farm, and Amy Readhead, tenant farmer of Crofts Field; Fiona Headley of Hertsmere District Council; Hazel Jones, Document Supply Librarian at the Institute of Engineering and Technology; Ron King, tenant farmer in Chingford; John Liddard and Christopher Smith, Thames Water; Mick Loades of Tobin Plant Ltd; Mike Matthews (www.boddyparts.co.uk); Mike Page (www.mike-page.co.uk); Simon Parry; Ray Rimell of Albatross Publications (www.windsockdatafilespecials.com); Kenny Roberts; Guy Smith; and Tony Preston (www.onesuffolk.co.uk/Thebertonpc).

Suggested Further Reading

Cole, C. and Cheesman, E.F., 1984, *The Air Defence of Britain, 1914–1918*, London, Putnam

Deighton, L. and Schwartzman, A., 1978, *Airshipwreck*, London, Book Club Associates

Evan-Hart, J., 2007, *War Torn Skies – Hertfordshire*, Walton on Thames, Red Kite

Fegan, T., 2002, *The 'Baby Killers': German Air Raids on Britain in the First World War*, Barnsley, Leo Cooper

Grosscup, B., 2006, *Strategic Terror: The Politics and Ethics of Aerial Bombardment*, London, Zed Books

Morris, J., 1993 (2nd ed.), *German Air Raids on Britain, 1914–1918*, Uckfield, Naval and Military Press

Poolman, K., 1975 (2nd ed.), *Zeppelins Over England*, London, White Lion Publishers

Rimell, R.L., 1984, *Zeppelin! A Battle for Air Supremacy in World War I*, London, Conway Maritime Press

Rimell, R. L., 2006, *The Last Flight of the L48*, Berkhamsted, Albatross Publications

Robinson, D., 1971 (3rd ed.), *The Zeppelin in Combat*, Henley-on-Thames, G.T. Foulis

Saunders, N.J., 2007, *Killing Time: Archaeology and the First World War*, Stroud, Sutton Publishing

Stephenson, C., 2004, *Zeppelins: German Airships, 1900–40*, Oxford, Osprey Publishing

Wells, H.G., 2005 (new ed.), *The War in the Air*, London, Penguin

Getting Involved

Membership of the Great War Archaeology Group is open to all. The group is formed of academics, digging archaeologists, metal-detectorists, students, and amateur enthusiasts. All work on a voluntary basis on field projects to investigate the material remains of the First World War.

Please email the GWAG Secretary, Julian Evan-Hart, if you would like to have your name added to the GWAG email list (j.evenhart@ntlworld.com). There is no charge, and you will receive notice of forthcoming GWAG activities. You can also consult the GWAG website (www.gwag.org).